ITALIAN

in 10 minutes a day®

by Kristine Kershul, M.A., University of California, Santa Barbara

Consultants: Susan Worthington   Karen Manarolla Nordquist

Bilingual Books, Inc.

1719 West Nickerson Street, Seattle, WA 98119

Tel: (206) 284-4211 Fax: (206) 284-3660

www.10minutesaday.com

Third printing, February 2004

Can you say this?

(keh) *(koh-sah)* *(eh)*
Che cosa è?
what   thing   is it

(eh) *(oo-nah)* *(pen-nah)*
È una penna.
it is   a   pen

(vor-reh-ee) *(oo-nah)* *(pen-nah)*
Vorrei una penna.
I would like

If you can say this, you can learn to speak Italian. You will be able to easily order wine, lunch, theater tickets, pastry, or anything else you wish. You simply ask **"Che cosa è?"** *(keh) (koh-sah) (eh)* and, upon learning what it is, you can order it with **"Vorrei quello"** *(vor-reh-ee) (kwel-loh)*. Sounds easy, doesn't it?

The purpose of this book is to give you an **immediate** speaking ability in Italian. Using the acclaimed *"10 minutes a day®"* methodology, you will acquire a large working vocabulary that will suit your needs, and you will acquire it almost automatically. To aid you, this book offers a unique and easy system of pronunciation above each word which walks you through learning Italian.

If you are planning a trip or moving to where Italian is spoken, you will be leaps ahead of everyone if you take just a few minutes a day to learn the easy key words that this book offers. Start with Step 1 and don't skip around. Each day, work as far as you can comfortably go in those 10 minutes. Don't overdo it. Some days you might want to just review. If you forget a word, you can always look it up in the glossary. Spend your first 10 minutes studying the map on the previous page. And yes, have fun learning your new language.

As you work through the Steps, always use the special features which only this series offers. This book contains sticky labels and flash cards, free words, puzzles and quizzes. When you have completed this book, cut out the menu guide and take it along on your trip.

Throughout this book you will find an easy pronunciation guide above all new words. Refer to this Step whenever you need help, but remember, spend no longer than 10 minutes a day.

Most letters in Italian are identical to those in English. Many Italian letters are pronounced just as they are in English, however, others are pronounced quite differently.

To learn the sounds of the Italian letters, here is the entire alphabet. Practice these sounds with the examples given which are mostly towns or areas in Italy which you might visit. You can always refer back to these pages if you need to review.

Italian letter	English sound	Examples	Write it here
a	ah	**Catania** *(kah-tahn-yah)*	_____
b	b	**Brindisi** *(breen-dee-zee)*	_____
c *(before a, o, u, and all consonants)*	k	**Como** *(koh-moh)*	_____
c *(before e, i)*	ch	**Cefalù** *(cheh-fah-loo)*	_____
ch	k	**Chianti** *(kee-ahn-tee)*	_____
ci *(before a, o, u)*	ch	**Francia** *(frahn-chah)* France	_____
d	d	**Dolomiti** *(doh-loh-mee-tee)*	_____
e	*(as in let)* eh	**Elba** *(el-bah)*	_____
f	f	**Firenze** *(fee-ren-tseh)*	_____
g *(before a, o, u)*	*(as in go)* g	**Garda** *(gar-dah)*	_____
g *(before e, i)*	*(as in John)* j	**Genova** *(jeh-noh-vah)*	_____
gh	*(as in spaghetti)* g	**Ghirla** *(geer-lah)*	_____
gi *(before a, o, u)*	*(as in John)* j	**Giarre** *(jar-reh)*	_____
gl	*(as in million)* l-y	**Puglia** *(pool-yah)*	_____
h	always silent	**Heraclea** *(eh-rah-kleh-ah)*	_____
i *(varies)*	ee	**Amalfi** *(ah-mahl-fee)*	_____
	yah	**Italia** *(ee-tahl-yah)*	_____
j	y	**Jesi** *(yeh-zee)*	_____
k	k	**Khamma** *(kahm-mah)*	_____

Letter	Sound	Example	Write it here
l	l	**L**ombardia (*lohm-bar-dee-ah*)	
m	m	**M**ilano (*mee-lah-noh*)	
n	n	**N**apoli (*nah-poh-lee*)	
o	oh	**O**rvieto (*or-vee-eh-toh*)	
p	p	**P**adova (*pah-doh-vah*)	
qu*	kw	**Qu**arazza (*kwah-rah-tsah*)	
r	(slightly rolled) r	**R**oma (*roh-mah*)	
s (*varies*)	z	**P**i**s**a (*pee-zah*)	Pisa, Pisa
	s	**S**iena (*see-eh-nah*)	
sc (*before a, o, u*)	sk	To**sc**ana (*toh-skah-nah*)	
sc (*before e, i*)	sh	**Sc**illa (*sheel-lah*)	
sch (*before e, i*)	sk	I**sch**ia (*eesk-yah*)	
sci (*before a, o, u*)	sh	Bre**sci**a (*breh-shah*)	
t	t	**T**orino (*toh-ree-noh*)	
u	oo	**U**mbria (*oom-bree-ah*)	
v	v	**V**enezia (*veh-neh-tsee-ah*)	
w	v	**W**elsberg (*velz-bairg*)	
x	ks	Colle di **X**omo (*kohl-leh*)(*dee*)(*ksoh-moh*)	
y	y	Courma**y**eur (*koor-my-yewr*)	
z (*varies*)	ts	La**z**io (*lah-tsee-oh*)	
	z	Vicen**z**a (*vee-chen-zah*)	
	dz	**Z**inola (*dzee-noh-lah*)	

Just as in English, "**q**" is always joined with the letter "**u**." The letter "**u**" is then silent.

Double consonants such as **tt**, **pp**, **mm** and **ll** are emphasized in Italian. Don't hesitate to over-exaggerate them.

Sometimes the phonetics may seem to contradict your pronunciation guide. Don't panic! The easiest and best possible phonetics have been chosen for each individual word. Pronounce the phonetics just as you see them. Don't over-analyze them. Speak with an Italian accent and, above all, enjoy yourself!

When you arrive in **Italia** *(ee-tahl-yah)* the very first thing you will need to do is ask questions — "Where (**dove**) *(doh-veh)* is the bus stop?" "**Dove** *(doh-veh)* can I exchange money?" "**Dove** *(doh-veh)* is the lavatory?" "**Dove** *(doh-veh)* is a restaurant?" "**Dove** *(doh-veh)* do I catch a taxi?" "**Dove** is a good hotel?" "**Dove** is my luggage?" — and the list will go on and on for the entire length of your visit. In Italian, there are SEVEN KEY QUESTION WORDS to learn. For example, the seven key question words will help you find out exactly what you are ordering in a restaurant before you order it — and not after the surprise (or shock!) arrives. Notice that only one letter is different in the Italian words for "what" and "who." Don't confuse them! Take a few minutes to study and practice saying the seven key question words listed below. Then cover the Italian with your hand and fill in each of the blanks with the matching **parola** *(pah-roh-lah)* **italiana.** *(ee-tahl-yah-nah)*

(doh-veh)
DOVE   =   WHERE *dove, dove, dove, dove*

(keh)
CHE   =   WHAT _____

(kee)
CHI   =   WHO _____

(pair-keh)
PERCHÈ   =   WHY _____

(kwahn-doh)
QUANDO   =   WHEN _____

(koh-meh)
COME   =   HOW _____

(kwahn-toh)
QUANTO   =   HOW MUCH _____

Now test yourself to see if you really can keep these **parole** *(pah-roh-leh)* straight in your mind. Draw lines between the Italian **e** *(eh)* and English equivalents below.

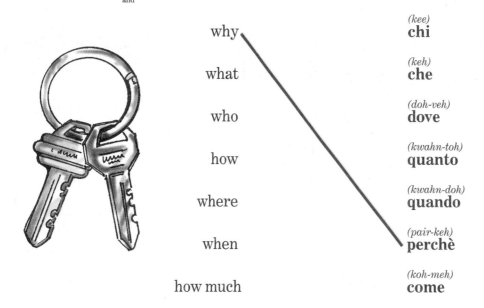

why	**chi** *(kee)*
what	**che** *(keh)*
who	**dove** *(doh-veh)*
how	**quanto** *(kwahn-toh)*
where	**quando** *(kwahn-doh)*
when	**perchè** *(pair-keh)*
how much	**come** *(koh-meh)*

Examine the following questions containing these **parole** *(pah-roh-leh)*. Practice the sentences out loud **e** *(eh)* and then practice by copying the Italian in the blanks underneath each question.

Che cosa è? *(keh) (koh-sah) (eh)*
What thing is it

Che cosa è?

Com'è l'insalata? *(koh-meh) (leen-sah-lah-tah)*
How is the salad

_____

Chi è? *(kee) (eh)*
Who is it

_____

Quando arriva il treno? *(kwahn-doh) (ar-ree-vah) (eel) (treh-noh)*
When arrives the train

_____

Quanto è? *(kwahn-toh) (eh)*
How much is it

_____

Dov'è il telefono? *(doh-veh) (eel) (teh-leh-foh-noh)*
Where is the telephone

_____

"Dove" *(doh-veh)* will be your most used question **parola**. Say each of the following Italian sentences aloud. Then write out each sentence without looking at the example. If you don't succeed on the first try, don't give up. Just practice each sentence until you are able to do it easily. Remember, **"ce"** is pronounced "cheh" and **"ci"** is pronounced "chee."

Dove sono i gabinetti?
(soh-noh) (ee) (gah-bee-net-tee)
Where   are   the   restrooms

Dov'è il tassì?
(doh-veh) (eel) (tahs-see)
Where   is   the   taxi

Dov'è l' autobus?
(doh-veh) (lah-oo-toh-boos)
Where   is   the bus

_____

Dov'è il tassì?

_____

Dov'è il ristorante?
(eel) (ree-stoh-rahn-teh)
the   restaurant

Dov'è la banca?
(lah) (bahn-kah)
the   bank

Dov'è l'albergo?
(lahl-bair-goh)
hotel

_____ _____ _____

Sì, you can see similarities between **inglese** *(een-gleh-zeh)* and **italiano** *(ee-tahl-yah-noh)* if you look closely. You will be
yes   English   Italian

amazed at the number of **parole** *(pah-roh-leh)* which are identical (or almost identical) in both languages.
words

Of course, they do not always sound the same when spoken by an Italian speaker, but the

similitudini *(see-mee-lee-too-dee-nee)* will certainly surprise you **e** *(eh)* make your work here easier. Listed below are five
similarities

"free" **parole** beginning with "**a**" *(ah)* to help you get started. Be sure to say each **parola** aloud **e** *(eh)*

then write out the **parole italiane** *(ee-tahl-yah-neh)* in the blanks to the right.
words   Italian

☑	**l'alcool** *(lahl-kohl)*	alcohol	*l'alcool, l'alcool, l'alcool, l'alcool*
❑	**le Alpi** *(leh)(ahl-pee)*	Alps	_____
❑	**americano** *(ah-meh-ree-kah-noh)*	American **a**	_____
❑	**l'animale** *(lah-nee-mah-leh)*	animal	_____
❑	**l'appartamento** *(lahp-par-tah-men-toh)*	apartment	_____

Free **parole** like these will appear at the bottom of the following pages in a yellow color band.

They are easy — enjoy them! Remember, in Italian, **"ch"** is pronounced "k."

(een) (ee-tahl-yah-noh)
In italiano   there are multiple **parole** for "the" and "a," but they are very easy. If the Italian
in   Italian   words

word ends in "**a**" (feminine) it *usually* will have the article "**la**." If the word ends in "**o**" (masculine)

it *usually* will have the article "**il**" or "**lo**." Study these patterns below.

(eel) (rah-gah-tsoh)
il ragazzo
the   boy

(ee) (rah-gah-tsee)
i ragazzi
the   boys

(lah) (rah-gah-tsah)
la ragazza
the   girl

(leh) (rah-gah-tseh)
le ragazze
the   girls

(loh) (spek-kee-oh)
lo specchio
the   mirror

(l-yee) (spek-kee)
gli specchi
the   mirrors

(oon) (seen-yoh-reh)
un signore
a   man

(deh-ee) (seen-yoh-ree)
dei signori
some   men

(oo-nah) (seen-yoh-rah)
una signora
a   lady

(del-leh) (seen-yoh-reh)
delle signore
some   ladies

(oo-noh) (strah-nee-eh-roh)
uno straniero
a   foreigner

(del-yee) (strah-nee-eh-ree)
degli stranieri
some   foreigners

(een-gleh-zeh)
This might appear difficult, but only because it is different from **inglese.** Just remember you will

be understood whether you say "**il ragazzo**" or "**la ragazzo**." Soon you will automatically select

the right one without even thinking about it.

In Step 2 you were introduced to the Seven Key

QuestionWords. These seven words are the basics, the

most essential building blocks for learning Italian.

Throughout this book you will come across keys

asking you to fill in the missing question word. Use

this opportunity not only to fill in the blank on that

key, but to review all your question words. Play with

the new sounds, speak slowly and have fun.

❑	**l'appetito** *(lahp-peh-tee-toh)*	appetite		_____
❑	**aprile** *(ah-pree-leh)*	April		_____
❑	**l'arrivo** *(lar-ree-voh)*	arrival	**a**	_____
❑	**l'attenzione** *(laht-ten-tsee-oh-neh)*	attention		_____
❑	**l'attore** *(laht-toh-reh)*	actor		

Before you proceed with this Step, situate yourself comfortably in your living room. Now look around you. Can you name the things that you see in this **stanza** *(stahn-zah)* (room) in Italian? You can probably guess **la lampada** *(lahm-pah-dah)* (lamp) and maybe even **il tavolo.** *(tah-voh-loh)* (table) Let's learn the rest of them. After practicing these **parole** out loud, write them in the blanks below.

(lahm-pah-dah)
la lampada_____
lamp

(soh-fah)
il sofà_____
sofa

(seh-dee-ah)
la sedia_____
chair

(tahp-peh-toh)
il tappeto_____
carpet

(tah-voh-loh)
il tavolo____il tavolo, il tavolo___
table

(por-tah)
la porta_____
door

(loh-roh-loh-joh)
l' orologio_____
clock

(ten-dee-nah)
la tendina_____
curtain

(teh-leh-foh-noh)
il telefono_____
telephone

(fee-neh-strah)
la finestra
window

_____

(kwah-droh)
il quadro
picture

_____

You will notice that the correct form of **il**, **la**, **l'** or **lo** *(eel)* is given **con** *(kohn)* (with) each noun. This is for your **informazione** *(een-for-mah-tsee-oh-neh)* (information) — just remember to use one of them. Now open your book to the sticky labels on page 17 and later on page 35. Peel off the first 11 labels **e** *(eh)* proceed around **la stanza,** *(stahn-zah)* (room) labeling these items in your home. This will help to increase your Italian **parola** power easily. Don't forget to say each **parola** as you attach the label.

Now ask yourself, **"Dov'è la lampada?"** *(doh-veh)* **e** *(eh)* point at it while you answer, **"Ecco la lampada."** *(ek-koh)* (here is)

Continue on down the **lista** *(lee-stah)* (list) above until you feel comfortable with these new **parole**.

❏	**la baia** *(bah-ee-ah)*	bay		_____
❏	**il balcone** *(bahl-koh-neh)*	balcony		_____
❏	**la banana** *(bah-nah-nah)*	banana	**b**	_____
❏	**la banca** *(bahn-kah)*	bank		_____
❏	**la benedizione** *(beh-neh-dee-tsee-oh-neh)*	benediction		_____

(lah) (kah-zah)
la casa = the house

(ek-koh)
Ecco la casa.
here is

(loof-fee-choh)
l' ufficio
office

(stahn-zah) *(bahn-yoh)*
la stanza da bagno
bathroom

(koo-chee-nah)
la cucina
kitchen

(kah-meh-rah) *(let-toh)*
la camera da letto
bedroom

(sah-lah) *(prahn-tsoh)*
la sala da pranzo
dining room

(sah-loht-toh)
il salotto
living room

(gah-rahzh)
il garage
garage

(kahn-tee-nah)
la cantina
basement

(pah-roh-leh)
While learning these new **parole,** let's not forget:

(lah-oo-toh) *(mahk-kee-nah)*
l' auto/ la macchina
automobile

(moh-toh-chee-klet-tah)
la motocicletta
motorcycle

(bee-chee-klet-tah)
la bicicletta
bicycle

_____

_____

_____

❑	**il biscotto** *(bee-skoht-toh)*	biscuit, cookie
❑	**la bistecca** *(bee-stek-kah)*	beefsteak
❑	**la bottiglia** *(boht-teel-yah)*	bottle
❑	**breve** *(breh-veh)*	brief, short
❑	**brillante** *(breel-lahn-teh)*	brilliant, shining

b

_____
_____
_____
_____
_____

(gaht-toh)
il gatto
cat

(jar-dee-noh)
il giardino
garden

(fee-oh-ree)
i fiori
flowers

_____

il giardino, il giardino

_____

(kah-neh)
il cane
dog

(boo-kah) (del-leh) (let-teh-reh)
la buca delle lettere
mailbox

(poh-stah)
la posta
mail

_____

_____

_____

(eh)
Peel off the next set of labels **e** wander through your **casa** *(kah-zah)* learning these new **parole**. *(pah-roh-leh)* It will

be somewhat difficult to label **il gatto,** *(gaht-toh)* cat **i fiori** *(fee-oh-ree)* flowers **o** *(oh)* or **il cane,** *(kah-neh)* dog but be creative. Practice by asking

yourself, **"Dov'è l'auto?"** *(lah-oo-toh)* car and reply, **"Ecco l'auto."** here is

Dov'è la casa?

(oo-noh) *(doo-eh)* *(treh)*
Uno, Due, Tre
one · two · three

Consider for a minute how important numbers are. How could you tell someone your phone number, your address **o** *(oh)* or your hotel room if you had no numbers? And think of how difficult it would be if you could not understand the time, the price of a cappuccino **o** the correct bus to take. When practicing the **numeri** *(noo-meh-ree)* numbers below, notice the similarities which have been underlined for you between **quattro** *(kwaht-troh)* four and **quattordici,** *(kwaht-tor-dee-chee)* fourteen **sette** *(set-teh)* seven and **diciassette** *(dee-chahs-set-teh)* seventeen **e** so on.

0	**zero** *(zeh-roh)*	_____
1	**uno** *(oo-noh)*	_____
2	**due** *(doo-eh)*	_____
3	**tre** *(treh)*	_____
4	**quattro** *(kwaht-troh)*	_____
5	**cinque** *(cheen-kweh)*	_____
6	**sei** *(seh-ee)*	_____
7	**sette** *(set-teh)*	*sette, sette, sette*
8	**otto** *(oht-toh)*	_____
9	**nove** *(noh-veh)*	_____
10	**dieci** *(dee-eh-chee)*	_____

10	**dieci** *(dee-eh-chee)*	_____
11	**undici** *(oon-dee-chee)*	_____
12	**dodici** *(doh-dee-chee)*	_____
13	**tredici** *(treh-dee-chee)*	_____
14	**quattordici** *(kwaht-tor-dee-chee)*	_____
15	**quindici** *(kween-dee-chee)*	_____
16	**sedici** *(seh-dee-chee)*	_____
17	**diciassette** *(dee-chahs-set-teh)*	_____
18	**diciotto** *(dee-choht-toh)*	_____
19	**diciannove** *(dee-chahn-noh-veh)*	_____
20	**venti** *(ven-tee)*	_____

☑ **la cerimonia** *(cheh-ree-moh-nee-ah)* . . . . ceremony · **c** · *la cerimonia, la cerimonia*
☐ **certo** *(chair-toh)* . . . . certainly · _____
☐ **il cinema** *(chee-neh-mah)* . . . . cinema, movie house · _____
☐ **il cioccolato** *(chohk-koh-lah-toh)* . . . . chocolate · _____
☐ **la comunicazione** *(koh-moo-nee-kah-tsee-oh-neh)* communication · _____

(oo-zee) **Usi** these *(noo-meh-ree)* **numeri** on a daily basis. Count to yourself **in** *(een)* **italiano** when you brush your teeth,
use   numbers   in   Italian

exercise **o** *(oh)* commute to work. Fill in the blanks below according to the **numeri** given in
numbers

parentheses. Now is also a good time to learn these two very important phrases.

(vor-reh-ee)
vorrei _____
I would like

(vor-rem-moh)
vorremmo _____
we would like

(vor-reh-ee)
Vorrei _____ (1)   *(bee-skoht-toh)* **biscotto.** biscuit   *(kwahn-tee)* **Quanti?** _____ (1) how many

Vorrei _____ (7)   *(frahn-koh-bohl-lee)* **francobolli.** stamps   **Quanti?** _____ (7)

(vor-reh-ee)
Vorrei _____ (8)   **francobolli.** stamps   **Quanti?** _____ (8)

Vorrei _____ (5)   **francobolli.**   **Quanti?** _cinque_ _____ (5)

(vor-rem-moh)
Vorremmo _____ (9)   *(kar-toh-lee-neh)* **cartoline.** postcards   **Quanti?** _____ (9)
we would like

Vorremmo _____ (10)   *(kar-toh-lee-neh)* **cartoline.**   *(kwahn-tee)* **Quanti?** _____ (10)
we would like

Vorrei _____ (1)   *(beel-yet-toh)* **biglietto.** ticket   **Quanti?** _____ (1)

(vor-rem-moh)
Vorremmo _____ (4)   *(beel-yet-tee)* **biglietti.** tickets   **Quanti?** _____ (4)

Vorremmo _____ (11)   *(beel-yet-tee)* **biglietti.**   **Quanti?** _____ (11)

(vor-reh-ee)
Vorrei _____ (3)   *(tah-tseh) (dee) (teh)* **tazze di tè.** cups of tea   **Quanti?** _____ (3)

Vorremmo _____ (4)   *(beek-kee-eh-ree)(dee)(ah-kwah)* **bicchieri di acqua.** glasses of water   _____ (4) (how many)

❏	**la conservazione** *(kohn-sair-vah-tsee-oh-neh)* ...	conservation	_____
❏	**la conversazione** *(kohn-vair-sah-tsee-oh-neh)* ...	conversation	_____
❏	**il coraggio** *(koh-rah-joh)*	courage **c**	_____
❏	**la cugina** *(koo-jee-nah)*	female cousin	_____
❏	**il cugino** *(koo-jee noh)*	male cousin	_____

Now see if you can translate the following thoughts into **italiano**. The answers are provided

(pah-jee-nah)

upside down at the bottom of the **pagina**.

page

1. I would like seven postcards.

_____

2. I would like nine stamps.

_____

3. We would like four cups of tea.

_____

4. We would like three tickets.

_____

Review **i numeri** 1 through 20. Write out your telephone number, fax number *(eh)* **e** cellular

number. Then write out a friend's telephone number and a relative's telephone number.

(2   0   6)   3   4   0 — 4   4   2   2

due zero sei _____

(_____) _____ _____ _____ — _____ _____ _____ _____

_____

(_____) _____ _____ _____ — _____ _____ _____ _____

_____

6   *(ee) (koh-loh-ree)*   I Colori
colors

(ee) (koh-loh-ree) (soh-noh)   *(een)(ee-tahl-yah)*   *(ah-meh-ree-kah)*
I colori sono the same **in Italia** as they are **in America** — they just have different
colors   are   in

(noh-mee)   *(vee-oh-let-toh)*
nomi. You can easily recognize **violetto** as violet. Let's learn the basic **colori** so when you are
names

(kah-zah)
invited to someone's **casa** **e** you want to bring flowers, you will be able to order the color you
house

want. Once you've learned **i colori,** quiz yourself. What color are your shoes? Your eyes?

Your hair? Your house?

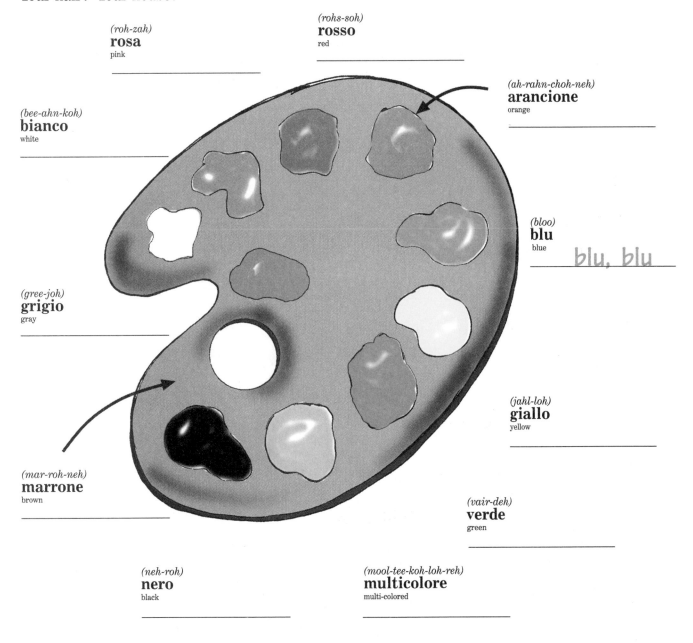

(roh-zah)
rosa
pink

(rohs-soh)
rosso
red

(ah-rahn-choh-neh)
arancione
orange

(bee-ahn-koh)
bianco
white

(bloo)
blu
blue

blu, blu

(gree-joh)
grigio
gray

(jahl-loh)
giallo
yellow

(mar-roh-neh)
marrone
brown

(vair-deh)
verde
green

(neh-roh)
nero
black

(mool-tee-koh-loh-reh)
multicolore
multi-colored

❑	**la danza** *(dahn-tsah)*	dance
❑	**decorato** *(deh-koh-rah-toh)*	decorated
❑	**delizioso** *(deh-lee-tsee-oh-zoh)*	delicious
❑	**denso** *(den-soh)*	dense
❑	**il desiderio** *(deh-zee-deh-ree-oh)*	desire, wish

d

Peel off the next group of labels **e** proceed to label these **colori** in your **casa.** Identify the two **o**
three dominant colors in the flags below.

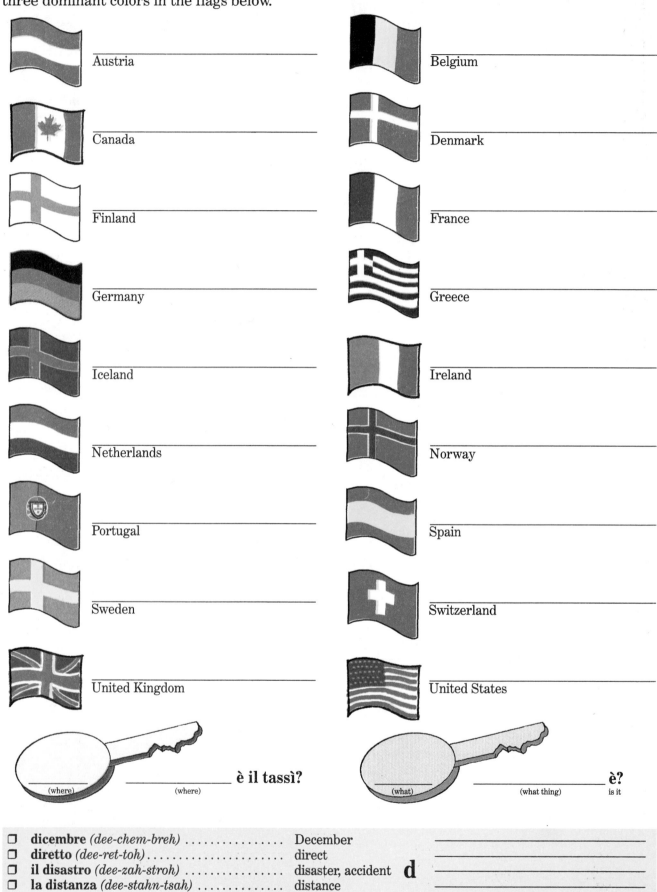

Austria _____

Belgium _____

Canada _____

Denmark _____

Finland _____

France _____

Germany _____

Greece _____

Iceland _____

Ireland _____

Netherlands _____

Norway _____

Portugal _____

Spain _____

Sweden _____

Switzerland _____

United Kingdom _____

United States _____

_____ _____ **è il tassì?**
(where)   (where)

_____ _____ **è?**
(what)   (what thing)   is it

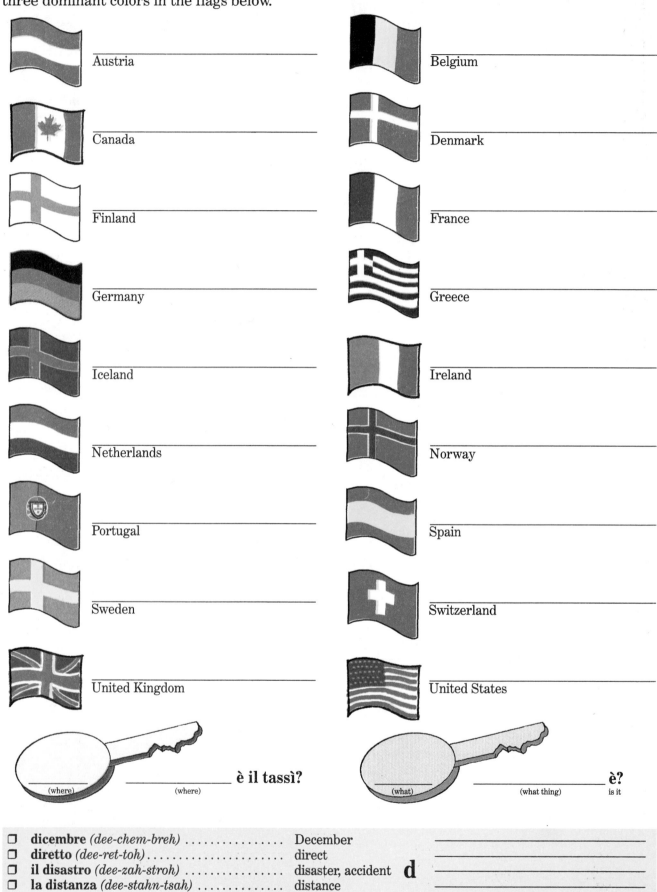

❑ **dicembre** *(dee-chem-breh)*	December	_____
❑ **diretto** *(dee-ret-toh)*	direct	_____
❑ **il disastro** *(dee-zah-stroh)*	disaster, accident **d**	_____
❑ **la distanza** *(dee-stahn-tsah)*	distance	_____
❑ **divino** *(dee-vee-noh)*	divine	_____

(lahm-pah-dah) **la lampada**	*(mahk-kee-nah)* **la macchina**	*(mar-roh-neh)* **marrone**	*(laht-teh)* **il latte**
(soh-fah) **il sofà**	*(moh-toh-chee-klet-tah)* **la motocicletta**	*(rohs-soh)* **rosso**	*(boor-roh)* **il burro**
(seh-dee-ah) **la sedia**	*(bee-chee-klet-tah)* **la bicicletta**	*(roh-zah)* **rosa**	*(sah-leh)* **il sale**
(tahp-peh-toh) **il tappeto**	*(gaht-toh)* **il gatto**	*(ah-rahn-choh-neh)* **arancione**	*(peh-peh)* **il pepe**
(tah-voh-loh) **il tavolo**	*(jar-dee-noh)* **il giardino**	*(bee-ahn-koh)* **bianco**	*(beek-kee-eh-reh) (vee-noh)* **il bicchiere da vino**
(por-tah) **la porta**	*(fee-oh-ree)* **i fiori**	*(jahl-loh)* **giallo**	*(beek-kee-eh-reh)* **il bicchiere**
(loh-roh-loh-joh) **l'orologio**	*(kah-neh)* **il cane**	*(gree-joh)* **grigio**	*(jor-nah-leh)* **il giornale**
(ten-dee-nah) **la tendina**	*(boo-kah) (del-leh) (let-teh-reh)* **la buca delle lettere**	*(neh-roh)* **nero**	*(tah-tsah)* **la tazza**
(teh-leh-foh-noh) **il telefono**	*(poh-stah)* **la posta**	*(bloo)* **blu**	*(kook-kee-eye-oh)* **il cucchiaio**
(fee-neh-strah) **la finestra**	*(zeh-roh)* **0 zero**	*(vair-deh)* **verde**	*(kohl-tel-loh)* **il coltello**
(kwah-droh) **il quadro**	*(oo-noh)* **1 uno**	*(mool-tee-koh-loh-reh)* **multicolore**	*(toh-vahl-yoh-loh)* **il tovagliolo**
(kah-zah) **la casa**	*(doo-eh)* **2 due**	*(bwohn) (jor-noh)* **buon giorno**	*(for-ket-tah)* **la forchetta**
(loof-fee-choh) **l'ufficio**	*(treh)* **3 tre**	*(bwoh-nah) (seh-rah)* **buona sera**	*(pee-aht-toh)* **il piatto**
(stahn-zah) (bahn-yoh) **la stanza da bagno**	*(kwaht-troh)* **4 quattro**	*(bwoh-nah) (noht-teh)* **buona notte**	*(lar-mah-dee-et-toh) (koo-chee-nah)* **l'armadietto di cucina**
(koo-chee-nah) **la cucina**	*(cheen-kweh)* **5 cinque**	*(chow)* **ciao**	*(teh)* **il tè**
(kah-meh-rah) (let-toh) **la camera da letto**	*(seh-ee)* **6 sei**	*(koh-meh) (vah)* **Come va?**	*(kahf-feh)* **il caffè**
(sah-lah) (prahn-tsoh) **la sala da pranzo**	*(set-teh)* **7 sette**	*(free-goh-ree-feh-roh)* **il frigorifero**	*(pah-neh)* **il pane**
(sah-loht-toh) **il salotto**	*(oht-toh)* **8 otto**	*(koo-chee-nah)* **la cucina**	*(pair) (fah-voh-reh)* **per favore**
(gah-rahzh) **il garage**	*(noh-veh)* **9 nove**	*(vee-noh)* **il vino**	*(grah-tsee-eh)* **grazie**
(kahn-tee-nah) **la cantina**	*(dee-eh-chee)* **10 dieci**	*(beer-rah)* **la birra**	*(mee) (skoo-zee)* **mi scusi**

STICKY LABELS

This book has over 150 special sticky labels for you to use as you learn new words. When you are introduced to one of these words, remove the corresponding label from these pages. Be sure to use each of these unique self-adhesive labels by adhering them to a picture, window, lamp, or whatever object they refer to. And yes, they are removable! The sticky labels make learning to speak Italian much more fun and a lot easier than you ever expected. For example, when you look in the mirror and see the label, say

(spek-kee-oh)
"lo specchio."
mirror ⟶

Don't just say it once, say it again and again. And once you label the refrigerator, you should never again open that door without saying

(free-goh-ree-feh-roh)
"il frigorifero."
refrigerator

By using the sticky labels, you not only learn new words, but friends and family learn along with you! The sooner you start, the sooner you can use these labels at home or work.

(eel) (deh-nah-roh)
Il Denaro
money

Before starting this Step, go back and review Step 5. It is important that you can count to

(ven-tee)
venti without looking at **il** *(lee-broh)* **libro.** Let's learn the larger *(noo-meh-ree)* **numeri** now. After practicing aloud
twenty   book

i numeri italiani below, write these **numeri** in the blanks provided. Again, notice the

(see-mee-lee-too-dee-nee)
similitudini (underlined) between **numeri** such as *(kwaht-troh)* **quattro** (4), *(kwaht-tor-dee-chee)* **quattordici** (14),

(kwah-rahn-tah) *(eh) (kwaht-troh-mee-lah)*
quaranta (40) **e quattromila** (4000).

10	*(dee-eh-chee)* **dieci** _____		1.000	*(meel-leh)* **mille** _____
20	*(ven-tee)* **venti** _____		2.000	*(doo-eh-mee-lah)* **duemila** _____
30	*(tren-tah)* **trenta** _trenta, trenta_		3.000	**tremila** _____
40	*(kwah-rahn-tah)* **quaranta** _____		4.000	**quattromila** _____
50	*(cheen-kwahn-tah)* **cinquanta** _____		5.000	**cinquemila** _____
60	*(ses-sahn-tah)* **sessanta** _____		6.000	**seimila** _____
70	*(set-tahn-tah)* **settanta** _____		7.000	**settemila** _____
80	*(oht-tahn-tah)* **ottanta** _____		8.000	**ottomila** _____
90	*(noh-vahn-tah)* **novanta** _____		9.000	**novemila** _____
100	*(chen-toh)* **cento** _____		10.000	*(dee-eh-chee-mee-lah)* **diecimila** _____
500	*(cheen-kweh-chen-toh)* **cinquecento** _____		10.500	**diecimila cinquecento** _____
1.000	*(meel-leh)* **mille** _____		11.000	*(oon-dee-chee-mee-lah)* **undicimila** _____

(ek-koh)
Ecco due important phrases to go with all these **numeri.** Say them out loud over and over and
here are

then write them out twice as many times.

(oh)
ho _____
I have

(ahb-bee-ah-moh)
abbiamo _____
we have

☐	**il dizionario** *(dee-tsee-oh-nah-ree-oh)*	dictionary	_____
☐	**il dollaro** *(dohl-lah-roh)*	dollar	_____
☐	**il dottore** *(doht-toh-reh)*	doctor	**d** _____
☐	**il dubbio** *(doob-bee-oh)*	doubt	_____
☐	**durante** *(doo-rahn-teh)*	during	_____

The unit of currency **in Italia** *(ee-tahl-yah)* **è** *(leh-oo-roh)* **l'euro,** abbreviated "**€**". Let's learn the various kinds of
in *is*

(moh-neh-teh) (eh) (beel-yet-tee)
monete e biglietti. Always be sure to practice each **parola** out loud. You might want to
coins   *bills*

(ah-des-soh)   *(kohn)*
exchange some money **adesso** so that you can familiarize yourself **con** the various types of
now   *with*

(deh-nah-roh)
denaro.
money

(beel-yet-tee)
Biglietti

(moh-neh-teh)
Monete

(cheen-kweh)(eh-oo-roh)
cinque euro

(dee-eh-chee)
dieci   euro

(ven-tee)
venti euro

(cheen-kwahn-tah)
cinquanta euro

(chen-toh)
cento euro
100

(ven-tee) (chen-teh-see-mee)
venti centesimi

(cheen-kwahn-tah)
cinquanta centesimi

(oon)(eh-oo-roh)
un euro

(doo-eh)
due euro

❏	**eccellente** *(eh-chel-len-teh)*	excellent
❏	**l'economia** *(leh-koh-noh-mee-ah)*	economy
❏	**l'entrata** *(len-trah-tah)*	entrance
❏	**est** *(est)*	east
❏	**Europa** *(eh-oo-roh-pah)*	Europe

e

Review **i numeri dieci** _(dee-eh-chee)_ through **mille** _(meel-leh)_ again. **Adesso,** _(ah-des-soh)_
now how do you say "twenty-two" **o**

"fifty-three" **in** _(een)_ **italiano?** Put the numbers together in a logical sequence just as you do in

English. See if you can say **e** write out **i numeri** on this **pagina.** _(pah-jee-nah)_
page **Le risposte** _(ree-spoh-steh)_ **sono** _(soh-noh)_
are at the

bottom of **la pagina.**

1. _____
    (25 = 20 + 5)

2. _____
    (83 = 80 + 3)

3. _____
    (47 = 40 + 7)

4. _____
    (96 = 90 + 6)

Adesso, _(ah-des-soh)_ how would you say the following **in italiano?**

5. _____
    (I have 8.000 lire.)

6. _____
    (We have 7.000 lire.)

To ask how much something costs **in italiano,** one asks — **Quanto** _(kwahn-toh)_ **costa?** _(koh-stah)_

Now you try it. _____
                  (How much does that cost?)

Answer the following questions based on the numbers in parentheses.

7. **Quanto** _(kwahn-toh)_ **costa?** _(koh-stah)_ **Costa** _(koh-stah)_
   (it) costs _____ (7) **euro.** _(eh-oo-roh)_

8. **Quanto costa il libro?** _(lee-broh)_
   book **Il libro costa** _____ (6) **euro.**

9. **Quanto costa il film?** _(feelm)_ **Il film costa** _____ (4) **euro.**

10. **Quanto costa la cartolina?** _(kar-toh-lee-nah)_
    postcard **La cartolina costa** _____ (2) **euro.**

(oh-jee) *(doh-mah-nee)* *(ee-eh-ree)*

Oggi, Domani e Ieri
today   tomorrow   and   yesterday

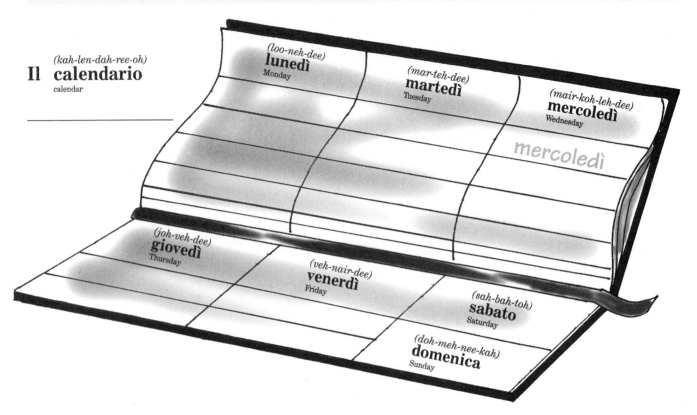

(kah-len-dah-ree-oh)

Il calendario
calendar

(loo-neh-dee)
lunedì
Monday

(mar-teh-dee)
martedì
Tuesday

(mair-koh-leh-dee)
mercoledì
Wednesday

mercoledì

(joh-veh-dee)
giovedì
Thursday

(veh-nair-dee)
venerdì
Friday

(sah-bah-toh)
sabato
Saturday

(doh-meh-nee-kah)
domenica
Sunday

Learn the days of the week by writing them in **il calendario** *(kah-len-dah-ree-oh)* above **e** then move on to the

(kwaht-troh)   *(jor-noh)*
quattro parts to each **giorno.**
four   day

(maht-tee-nah)
la mattina
morning

(poh-meh-ree-joh)
il pomeriggio
afternoon

(seh-rah)
la sera
evening

(noht-teh)
la notte
night

☐ **la famiglia** *(fah-meel-yah)* .... family
☐ **famoso** *(fah-moh-zoh)* .... famous   **f** _____
☐ **la farmacia** *(far-mah-chee-ah)* .... pharmacy, drugstore _____
☐ **il favore** *(fah-voh-reh)* .... favor _____
☐ **– per favore** *(pair)(fah-voh-reh)* .... please _____

È molto importante *(mohl-toh)* *(eem-por-tahn-teh)* to know the days of the week **e** the various parts of the day as well as

it is very   important

these **tre parole.**

(ee-eh-ree)
ieri

(oh-jee)
oggi

(doh-mah-nee)
domani

(loo-neh-dee)
lunedì
Monday

(mar-teh-dee)
martedì
Tuesday

(mair-koh-leh-dee)
mercoledì
Wednesday

(joh-veh-dee)
giovedì
Thursday

(veh-nair-dee)
venerdì
Friday

(sah-bah-toh)
sabato
Saturday

(doh-meh-nee-kah)
domenica
Sunday

(keh) *(jor-noh)* *(oh-jee)*
Che giorno è oggi?_____

what   day   is

Che giorno è domani?_____

(eh-rah) *(ee-eh-ree)*
Che giorno era ieri? _____

was

(oh-jee)
Oggi è mercoledì, sì? So, _____

yes   (tomorrow)

è giovedì e _____ **era martedì. Gli Italiani** begin counting their

(yesterday)   was   the   Italians

(eh-rah)   *(l-yee)* *(ee-tahl-yah-nee)*

(set-tee-mah-nah)   *(loo-neh-dee)*   *(set-tee-mah-nah)*
settimana on Monday with **lunedì.** In Italian, the days of the **settimana** are not capitalized

week   week

as **in inglese.**

a. Sunday morning   = _____

b. Friday morning   = _____

c. Saturday evening   = _____

d. Thursday afternoon   = _____

e. Thursday evening   = _____

f. yesterday evening   = _____

g. tomorrow afternoon   = _____

h. tomorrow evening   = _____

_____ _____ **è il concerto?**

(when) (when)

(kohn-chair-toh)
concerto
concert

_____ _____ **è?**

(who) (who)

is it

23

Knowing the parts of **il giorno** *(jor-noh)* day will help you to learn the various **saluti** *(sah-loo-tee)* **italiani** *(ee-tahl-yah-nee)* greetings below.

Practice these every day until your trip.

(bwohn) (jor-noh)
buon giorno _____
good morning/good day

(bwoh-nah) (seh-rah)
buona sera _____
good   evening

(bwoh-nah) (noht-teh)
buona notte _____
good   night

(chow)
ciao _____
hi!/bye!

Take the next **quattro** *(kwah-troh)* four labels **e** stick them on the appropriate **cose** *(koh-zeh)* things in your **casa.** house Make sure you attach them to the correct items, as they are only **in italiano.** How about the bathroom mirror **per "buon giorno"?** *(pair) (bwohn) (jor-noh)* for **o** your alarm clock **per "buona notte"?** *(pair) (bwoh-nah) (noht-teh)* Let's not forget,

(koh-meh) (vah)
Come va? _____
How are you

Now for some " **sì** *(see)* yes " or " **no** *(no)* no " questions –

Are your eyes **blu?** *(bloo)* _____   Are your shoes **marroni?** *(mar-roh-nee)* _____

Is your favorite color **rosso?** *(rohs-soh)* _____   Is today **sabato?** *(sah-bah-toh)* _____

Do you own a **cane?** *(kah-neh)* _____   Do you own a **gatto?** *(gaht-toh)* _____

You **è** are about one-fourth of your way through this **libro** *(lee-broh)* book and it is a good time to quickly review

le parole you have learned before doing the crossword puzzle on the next **pagina.**

Buon divertimento e buona fortuna. *(bwohn)* *(dee-vair-tee-men-toh)* *(for-too-nah)* have fun   good   luck

CROSSWORD PUZZLE (PAROLE CROCIATE)
(kroh-chah-teh)

ACROSS

1. I would like
2. dog
3. gray
4. man
5. nine
6. garden
7. Sunday
8. with
9. coin
10. five
11. money
12. black
13. yellow
14. who
15. day
16. green
17. Italy
18. clock
19. three
21. how much
22. multi-colored
23. evening
24. today
25. why
26. night
27. here is / are
28. we have

DOWN

1. Friday
2. yesterday
3. cousin
4. chair
5. Saturday
6. nineteen
7. afternoon
8. water
9. bank
10. postcard
11. where
13. hi! / bye!
14. what is it (what thing is it)
15. salad
16. twenty
17. white
19. curtain
20. lamp
21. four
22. Tuesday
23. two
24. red
25. how

☐ **il filtro** *(feel-troh)* . . . . filter _____

☐ **finalmente** *(fee-nahl-men-teh)* . . . . finally _____

☐ **finito** *(fee-nee-toh)* . . . . finished, ended **f** _____

☐ **la fontana** *(fohn-tah-nah)* . . . . fountain _____

☐ **la forchetta** *(for-ket-tah)* . . . . fork _____

(een) *(dah)* *(soh-prah)*

In, da, sopra . . .

in   from   over

(preh-poh-zee-tsee-oh-nee)

Le preposizioni **italiane** (words like "in," "on," "through" and "next to") **sono** easy to
prepositions   are

learn, **e** they allow you to be precise **con** a minimum of effort. Instead of having to point **sei** *(seh-ee)*

times at a piece of yummy pastry you would like, you can explain precisely which one you want

by saying **è** *(eh)* behind, in front of, next to **o** under the piece of pastry that the salesperson is
it is

starting to pick up. Let's learn some of these **piccole parole.** *(peek-koh-leh)*
                                                                little

(soht-toh)
sotto_____
under

(een)   *(nel-lah)*
in (also seen as **nel, nella**) _____
into/in   in the

(soh-prah)
sopra _____
over

(dah-vahn-tee) *(dah-vahn-tee)* *(ahl)*
davanti a/davanti al_____
in front   of in front   of the

(frah)
fra_____
between

(dee-eh-troh)
dietro_____
behind

(ahk-kahn-toh) *(ah)* *(ahk-kahn-toh)* *(ahl)*
accanto a/ accanto al _____
next   to   next   to the

(dah)   *(dahl)* *(dahl-lah)*
da (also seen as **dal, dalla**) _____
of/from   from the

(soo) *(sool)* *(sool-lah)*
su (sul, sulla)_____
on   on the

(dohl-cheh)
il dolce _____
pastry!

When followed by "the," many of these **piccole parole** join together with "the" and change their

forms slightly.

(vah)
_____ **va?**
(how)   (how)   are you

(tahs-see) *(jahl-loh)*
_____ **è il tassì giallo?**
(why)   (why)   yellow

❑	**la foresta** *(foh-reh-stah)*	forest	_____
❑	**la forma** *(for-mah)*	form	_____
❑	**Francia** *(frahn-chah)*	France	_____
❑	**fresco** *(freh-skoh)*	cool, fresh	_____
❑	**la frutta** *(froot-tah)*	fruit	_____

f

Il *(dohl-cheh)* **dolce è** _____ *(tah-voh-loh)* **tavolo.**
pastry   (on + the)   table

Il *(kah-neh)* **cane nero è** _____ **il tavolo.**
dog   (under)   table

Il *(meh-dee-koh)* **medico è** _____ *(ahl-bair-goh)* **buon albergo.**
doctor   (in + the)   hotel

Dov'è il medico? _____

Il *(seen-yoh-reh)* **signore è** _____ **albergo.**
man   (in front of + the)

Dov'è il signore? _____

Il *(teh-leh-foh-noh)* **telefono è** _____ *(kwah-droh)* **quadro.**
telephone   (next to + the)   picture

Dov'è il telefono? _____

(ah-des-soh) **Adesso,** fill in each blank on the picture below with the best possible one of these *(peek-koh-leh)* **piccole**
now   little

parole. One of the many sights you might see could be **il** *(pohn-teh) (vek-kee-oh)* **Ponte Vecchio.** Do you recognize it
old bridge in Florence

in the picture below?

_____
(over)

(in)

(behind)

(under)

(between)

(in front of)

(jen-ny-oh) *(feb-bry-oh)* *(mar-tsoh)*
Gennaio, Febbraio, Marzo
January   February   March

You have learned the days of **la settimana,** *(set-tee-mah-nah)* week, so now **è il momento** *(moh-men-toh)* it is moment to learn **i mesi dell'anno** *(meh-zee) (del-lahn-noh)* months of the year **e** all the different kinds of **tempo.** *(tem-poh)* weather

(jen-ny-oh) **gennaio**	*(feb-bry-oh)* **febbraio**

(jen-ny-oh) **gennaio** | *(feb-bry-oh)* **febbraio** | *(mar-tsoh)* **marzo** | *(ah-pree-leh)* **aprile**

(mah-joh) **maggio** | *(joon-yoh)* **giugno** | *(lool-yoh)* **luglio** | *(ah-goh-stoh)* **agosto**

(set-tem-breh) **settembre** | *(oht-toh-breh)* **ottobre** | *(noh-vem-breh)* **novembre** | *(dee-chem-breh)* **dicembre**

When someone asks, "**Che tempo fa oggi?**" *(keh)* what *(fah)* is the weather *(oh-jee)* making today you have a variety of answers. Let's learn them but first, does this sound familiar?

Trenta giorni ha settembre, aprile, giugno e novembre... *(ah)* *(set-tem-breh)* has *(ah-pree-leh)* *(joon-yoh)* *(noh-vem-breh)*

- ☐ **il giardino** *(jar-dee-noh)* .... garden
- ☐ **giugno** *(joon-yoh)* .... June
- ☐ **il governo** *(goh-vair-noh)* .... government   **g**
- ☐ **grande** *(grahn-deh)* .... big, large, grand
- ☐ **la guida** *(gwee-dah)* .... guide

(keh) *(oh-jee)*
Che tempo fa oggi? _____
what   today

(neh-vee-kah)
Nevica in gennaio. _____
it snows   in

(ahn-keh)
Nevica anche in febbraio. _____
     also

(pee-oh-veh)
Piove in marzo. _____
it rains

(ahn-keh)
Piove anche in aprile. _____
    also

(tee-rah) *(ven-toh)* *(mah-joh)*
Tira vento in maggio. _____
it's   windy

(cheh) *(soh-leh)* *(joon-yoh)*
C'è sole in giugno. _____
there is   sun

(lool-yoh)
C'è sole anche in luglio. _____

(fah) *(kahl-doh)*
Fa caldo in agosto. _____
it makes warm/hot

Fa bel tempo in settembre. _____
    nice

(freh-skoh)
Fa fresco in ottobre. _____
  cool

(kaht-tee-voh)
Fa cattivo tempo in novembre. _____
   bad

(fred-doh)
Fa freddo in dicembre. _____
   cold

(keh)
Che tempo fa in febbraio? _____

Che tempo fa in aprile? _____

Che tempo fa in maggio? _____

Che tempo fa in settembre? _____

❐	**incantevole** *(een-kahn-teh-voh-leh)*	enchanting, charming	_____
❐	**indispensabile** *(een-dee-spen-sah-bee-leh)* . .	indispensable	_____
❐	**l'individuo** *(leen-dee-vee-doo-oh)*	individual (person) **i**	_____
❐	**l'industria** *(leen-doo-stree-ah)*	industry	_____
❐	**industrioso** *(een-doo-stree-oh-zoh)*	industrious	_____

Adesso for **le stagioni** *(stah-joh-nee)* **dell'anno** *(del-lahn-noh)* . . .
of the year

(leen-vair-noh)
l'inverno
winter

(leh-stah-teh)
l'estate
summer

(lah-oo-toon-noh)
l'autunno
autumn

(pree-mah-veh-rah)
la primavera
spring

(chen-tee-grah-doh)
Centigrado
Centigrade

(fah-ren-heit)
Fahrenheit
Fahrenheit

°C | °F
100 | 212
37 | 98.6
20 | 68
0 | 32
-17.8 | 0
-23.3 | -10

(grah-dee)
gradi
degrees

At this point, **è una buona idea** *(eh) (bwoh-nah) (ee-deh-ah)* to familiarize
good
yourself **con le temperature europee.** *(tem-peh-rah-too-reh) (eh-oo-roh-peh-eh)*
temperatures European
(tair-moh-meh-troh)
Carefully study **il termometro** because **le**

temperature in Europa *(ee-oo-roh-pah)* are calculated on the

basis of Centigrade (not Fahrenheit).

To convert °F to °C, subtract 32 and multiply by 0.55.

98.6 °F - 32 = 66.6 x 0.55 = 37 °C

To convert °C to °F, multiply by 1.8 and add 32.

37 °C x 1.8 = 66.6 + 32 = 98.6 °F

What is normal body temperature in **Centigrado?**

What is the freezing point in **Centigrado?**

☐ **l'influenza** *(leen-floo-en-tsah)* . . . . influence
☐ **l'informazione** *(leen-for-mah-tsee-oh-neh)* . . . information
☐ **l'ingegnere** *(leen-jen-yeh-reh)* . . . . engineer   **i**
☐ **l'Inghilterra** *(leen-gheel-tair-rah)* . . . . England
☐ **innamorato** *(een-nah-moh-rah-toh)* . . . . enamored, in love

11   Famiglia, Fame, e Fede
(fah-meel-yah) *(fah-meh)* *(feh-deh)*
family   hunger   faith

Just as we have the three "R's" **in inglese, in italiano** there are the three **"F's"** (**famiglia,** *(fah-meel-yah)*

fame e fede) which help us to understand some of the basics of **la vita italiana.**   Study the
(fah-meh) *(feh-deh)*   *(vee-tah)* *(ee-tahl-yah-nah)*
                                              life   Italian

family tree below.

(Signora Bianchi)
Claudia Bianchi
la nonna
grandmother

(Signor Bianchi)
Paolo Bianchi
il nonno
grandfather

Nicola Bianchi
il padre
father

(Signora Manfredi)
Sandra Bianchi Manfredi
la zia
aunt

(Signor Manfredi)
Filippo Manfredi
lo zio
uncle

Maria Rizzo Bianchi
la madre
mother

(Signor Bianchi)
Giovanni Bianchi
il figlio
son

(Signorina Bianchi)
Elena Bianchi
la figlia
daughter

☐ **l'insalata** *(leen-sah-lah-tah)* . . . . salad
☐ **interamente** *(een-teh-rah-men-teh)* . . . . . . entirely
☐ **interessante** *(een-teh-res-sahn-teh)* . . . . interesting
☐ **l'invito** *(leen-vee-toh)* . . . . invitation
☐ **l'isola** *(lee-zoh-lah)* . . . . island

i

_____
_____
_____
_____
_____

Let's learn how to identify **la famiglia** by **nome**. Study the following **esempi** carefully.

(fah-meel-yah) family   _(noh-meh)_ name   _(eh-zem-pee)_ examples

(koh-meh) (see) (kee-ah-mah)
Come si chiama? _____
what is your name/how are you called

(mee) (kee-ah-moh)
Mi chiamo _____
my name is/I am called   (your name)

(jeh-nee-toh-ree)
i genitori
parents

(pah-dreh)
il padre _____
father

(kee-ah-mah)
Come si chiama il padre? _____
how   is called   the father

(mah-dreh)
la madre _____
mother

Come si chiama la madre? _____
how   is called   mother

(feel-yee)
i figli
children

(feel-yoh) _(feel-yah)_ _(frah-tel-loh)_ _(soh-rel-lah)_
il figlio e la figlia = fratello e sorella
                                      brother   sister

(feel-yoh)
il figlio _____
son

(kee-ah-mah) _(feel-yoh)_
Come si chiama il figlio? _____
son

(feel-yah)
la figlia _____
daughter

(see) _(feel-yah)_
Come si chiama la figlia? _____
daughter

(pah-ren-tee)
i parenti
relatives

(nohn-noh)
il nonno _____
grandfather

(koh-meh)
Come si chiama il nonno? _____
grandfather

(nohn-nah)
la nonna _____
grandmother

(kee-ah-mah)
Come si chiama la nonna? _____
grandmother

Now you ask —

_____
(How are you called?/What is your name?)

And answer —

_____
(My name is . . .)

❑	**il lago** _(lah-goh)_	lake	_____
❑	**largo** _(lar-goh)_	wide, broad	_____
❑	**il legume** _(leh-goo-meh)_	vegetable	_____
❑	**la lettera** _(let-teh-rah)_	letter	_____
❑	**la lezione** _(leh-tsee-oh-neh)_	lesson, lecture	_____

l

La Cucina
(koo-chee-nah)
kitchen

il frigorifero
(free-goh-ree-feh-roh)
refrigerator

_____

la cucina
(koo-chee-nah)
stove

_____

il burro
(boor-roh)
butter

_____

il vino
(vee-noh)
wine

_____

il latte
(laht-teh)
milk

_____

la birra
(beer-rah)
beer

_____

Answer these questions aloud.

Dov'è la birra? *(beer-rah)* beer . . . . **La birra è nel frigorifero.** *(free-goh-ree-feh-roh)* in the

Dov'è il latte? milk   **Dov'è il vino ?** wine   **Dov'è il burro?** butter

Adesso apra *(ah-prah)* open your **libro** *(lee-broh)* book to the **pagina con** the labels **e** remove the next group of labels **e**

proceed to label all these **cose** *(koh-zeh)* things in your **cucina.** *(koo-chee-nah)* kitchen

❑	**libero** *(lee-beh-roh)*	free, liberated	_____
❑	**la lingua** *(leen-gwah)*	language	_____
❑	**la lista** *(lee-stah)*	list	_____
❑	**la lotteria** *(loht-teh-ree-ah)*	lottery	_____
❑	**lungo** *(loon-goh)*	long	_____

l

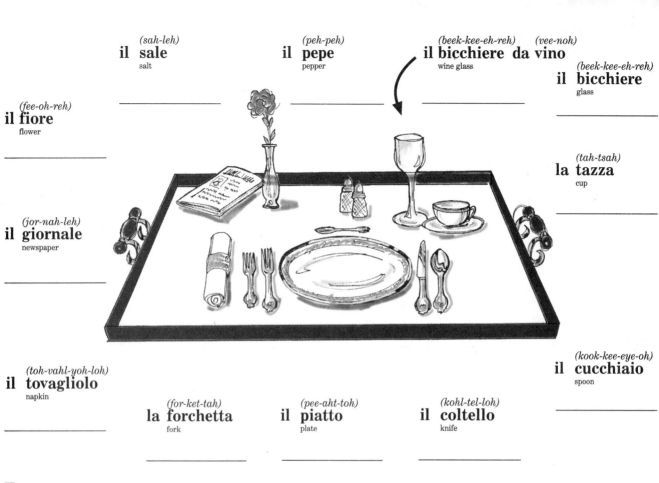

(sah-leh)
il sale
salt

_____

(peh-peh)
il pepe
pepper

_____

(beek-kee-eh-reh) *(vee-noh)*
il bicchiere da vino
wine glass

_____

(beek-kee-eh-reh)
il bicchiere
glass

_____

(fee-oh-reh)
il fiore
flower

_____

(tah-tsah)
la tazza
cup

_____

(jor-nah-leh)
il giornale
newspaper

_____

(toh-vahl-yoh-loh)
il tovagliolo
napkin

_____

(kook-kee-eye-oh)
il cucchiaio
spoon

_____

(for-ket-tah)
la forchetta
fork

_____

(pee-aht-toh)
il piatto
plate

_____

(kohl-tel-loh)
il coltello
knife

_____

E more . . .

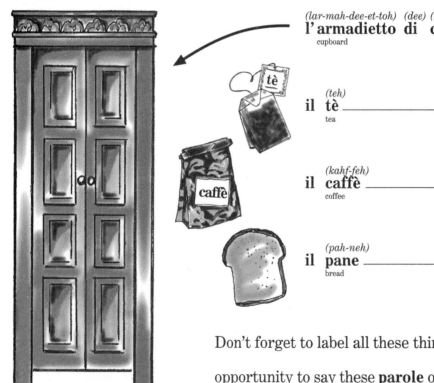

(lar-mah-dee-et-toh) *(dee)* *(koo-chee-nah)*
l'armadietto di cucina _____
cupboard

(teh)
il tè _____
tea

(doh-veh)
Dov'è il tè?

(nel-lar-mah-dee-et-toh)
Il tè è nell'armadietto.

(kahf-feh)
il caffè _____
coffee

Dov'è il caffè?

(pah-neh)
il pane _____
bread

Dov'è il pane?

Don't forget to label all these things and do not forget to use every

opportunity to say these **parole** out loud. **È molto importante.**
(eem-por-tahn-teh)
very

☐ **il maestro** *(mah-eh-stroh)* . . . . master, teacher _____
☐ **magnifico** *(mahn-yee-fee-koh)* . . . . magnificent _____
☐ **la maniera** *(mah-nee-eh-rah)* . . . . manner, way **m** _____
☐ **marzo** *(mar-tsoh)* . . . . March _____
☐ **il matrimonio** *(mah-tree-moh-nee-oh)* . . . . . marriage, wedding _____

(preh-goh) **prego**	*(frahn-koh-bohl-loh)* **il francobollo**	*(pet-tee-neh)* **il pettine**	*(short)* **i short**
(let-toh) **il letto**	*(kar-toh-lee-nah)* **la cartolina**	*(soh-prah-bee-toh)* **il soprabito**	*(mahl-yet-tah)* **la maglietta**
(koo-shee-noh) **il cuscino**	*(pahs-sah-por-toh)* **il passaporto**	*(lohm-brel-loh)* **l'ombrello**	*(moo-tahn-deh)* **le mutande**
(koh-pair-tah) **la coperta**	*(beel-yet-toh)* **il biglietto**	*(leem-pair-meh-ah-bee-leh)* **l'impermeabile**	*(kah-noht-tee-eh-rah)* **la canottiera**
(zvel-yah) **la sveglia**	*(vah-lee-jah)* **la valigia**	*(gwahn-tee)* **i guanti**	*(veh-stee-toh)* **il vestito**
(spek-kee-oh) **lo specchio**	*(bor-sah)* **la borsa**	*(kahp-pel-loh)* **il cappello**	*(kah-mee-chet-tah)* **la camicetta**
(lah-vahn-dee-noh) **il lavandino**	*(por-tah-fohl-yoh)* **il portafoglio**	*(kahp-pel-loh)* **il cappello**	*(gohn-nah)* **la gonna**
(ah-shoo-gah-mah-nee) **gli asciugamani**	*(deh-nah-roh)* **il denaro**	*(stee-vah-lee)* **gli stivali**	*(mahl-yah)* **la maglia**
(vee-chee) **il W.C.**	*(kar-teh)* *(kreh-dee-toh)* **le carte di credito**	*(skar-peh)* **le scarpe**	*(soht-toh-veh-steh)* **la sottoveste**
(doh-chah) **la doccia**	*(trah-vel)* *(check)* **i travel check**	*(skar-peh)* *(ten-nees)* **le scarpe da tennis**	*(reh-jee-pet-toh)* **il reggipetto**
(mah-tee-tah) **la matita**	*(mahk-kee-nah)* *(foh-toh-grah-fee-kah)* **la macchina fotografica**	*(lah-bee-toh)* **l'abito**	*(moo-tahn-deh)* **le mutande**
(teh-leh-vee-zoh-reh) **il televisore**	*(pel-lee-koh-lah)* **la pellicola**	*(krah-vaht-tah)* **la cravatta**	*(kahl-tsee-nee)* **i calzini**
(pen-nah) **la penna**	*(koh-stoo-meh)* *(bahn-yoh)* **il costume da bagno**	*(kah-mee-chah)* **la camicia**	*(kahl-tseh)* **le calze**
(ree-vee-stah) **la rivista**	*(sahn-dah-lee)* **i sandali**	*(fah-tsoh-let-toh)* **il fazzoletto**	*(pee-jah-mah)* **il pigiama**
(lee-broh) **il libro**	*(ohk-kee-ah-lee)* *(soh-leh)* **gli occhiali da sole**	*(jahk-kah)* **la giacca**	*(kah-mee-chah)* *(noht-teh)* **la camicia da notte**
(kohm-pyoo-tair) **il computer**	*(spah-tsoh-lee-noh)* *(den-tee)* **lo spazzolino da denti**	*(pahn-tah-loh-nee)* **i pantaloni**	*(lahk-kahp-pah-toy-oh)* **l'accappatoio**
(ohk-kee-ah-lee) **gli occhiali**	*(den-tee-free-choh)* **il dentifricio**	*(jeans)* **i jeans**	*(pahn-toh-foh-leh)* **le pantofole**
(kar-tah) **la carta**	*(sah-poh-neh)* **il sapone**	*(ven-goh)* *(dahl-yee)* *(stah-tee)* *(oo-nee-tee)* **Vengo dagli Stati Uniti.**	
(cheh-stee-noh) **il cestino**	*(rah-zoy-oh)* **il rasoio**	*(vor-reh-ee)* *(eem-pah-rah-reh)* *(lee-tahl-yah-noh)* **Vorrei imparare l'italiano.**	
(let-teh-rah) **la lettera**	*(deh-oh-doh-rahn-teh)* **il deodorante**	*(mee)* *(kee-ah-moh)* **Mi chiamo _____.**	

PLUS...

This book includes a number of other innovative features unique to the **"10 minutes a day®"** series. At the back of this book you will find twelve pages of flash cards. Cut them out and flip through them at least once a day.

On pages 116, 117 and 118 you will find a beverage guide and a menu guide. Don't wait until your trip to use them. Clip out the menu guide and use it tonight at the dinner table. Take them both with you the next time you dine at your favorite Italian restaurant.

By using the special features in this book, you will be speaking Italian before you know it.

(bwohn)   *(dee-vair-tee-men-toh)*
Buon divertimento!
have fun

(kee-eh-zah)
La Chiesa
church

In Italia there is not the wide variety of *(reh-lee-joh-nee)* **religioni** that *(ahb-bee-ah-moh)* **abbiamo** *(kwee)* **qui** in
religions · we have · here

(ah-meh-ree-kah)
America.   A person **è** *(jeh-neh-rahl-men-teh)* **generalmente** one of the following.
generally

1. *(kaht-toh-lee-koh)* *(kaht-toh-lee-kah)*
   cattolico / cattolica _____
   Catholic (♂)   Catholic (♀)

2. *(proh-teh-stahn-teh)*
   protestante _____
   Protestant (♂) or (♀)

3. *(eh-breh-oh)(eh-breh-ah)*
   ebreo / ebrea _____
   Jewish (♂)   Jewish (♀)

(ek-koh)   *(kaht-teh-drah-leh)*
Ecco una cattedrale in Italia.
here is   cathedral

(eh)
È una cattedrale *(kaht-toh-lee-kah)* **cattolica?**
is it

È una cattedrale *(noo-oh-vah)* **nuova?**
new

È una cattedrale *(vek-kee-ah)* **vecchia?**
old

È una cattedrale *(bel-lah)* **bella?**
beautiful

(mohl-teh) (bel-leh) (kaht-teh-drah-lee)
You will see **molte belle cattedrali** like this during your holiday **in Italia.**   **Adesso,** let's
many   beautiful   now

learn how to say "I am" **in italiano:** *(ee-oh) (soh-noh)* **io sono** _____
                                         I   am

To make an adjective feminine **in italiano,** you usually change the **"o"** at the end to an **"a."**

Adjectives that end in **"e"** can be either masculine or feminine. Test yourself — write each

sentence on the next page for more practice. Add your own personal variations as well.

(how much)   _____ **è?**
            (how much)   is it

❏	**il medico** *(meh-dee-koh)*	doctor, physician	_____
❏	**la memoria** *(meh-moh-ree-ah)*	memory	_____
❏	**meno** *(meh-noh)*	minus, less	**m** _____
❏	**meraviglioso** *(meh-rah-veel-yoh-zoh)*	marvelous	_____
❏	**il mercato** *(mair-kah-toh)*	market	_____

37

(ee-oh) (soh-noh) (kaht-toh-lee-koh)
Io sono cattolico. _____
I am Catholic (♠)

(proh-teh-stahn-teh)
Io sono protestante. _____

(eh-breh-oh)
Io sono ebreo. _____
Jewish (♠)

(ah-meh-ree-kah-noh)
Io sono americano. _____
American (♠)

(eh-oo-roh-pah)
Io sono in Europa. _____
Europe

(kah-nah-deh-zeh)
Io sono canadese. _____
Canadian

(kee-eh-zah)
Io sono nella chiesa. _____
I am in the church

Io sono in Italia. _____

(kaht-toh-lee-kah)
Io sono cattolica. _____
Catholic (♀)

(see-chee-lee-ah)
Io sono in Sicilia. _____
Sicily

(nel-lahl-bair-goh)
Io sono nell'albergo. _____
in the hotel

(ree-stoh-rahn-teh)
Io sono nel ristorante. _____
in the

Io sono nella cucina. _____
in the kitchen

(stahn-koh)
Io sono stanco. _____
tired

(nohn)
To negate any of these statements, simply add "**non**" before the verb.
not/no

(nohn)
Io non sono protestante. _____
not

(stahn-koh)
Io non sono stanco. _____
not tired

Go through and drill these sentences again but with "**non**."

(fah-meel-yah)
Adesso, take a piece of paper. Our **famiglia** from earlier had a reunion. Identify everyone

(kor-ret-tah)
below by writing **la parola italiana corretta** for each person — **la madre, lo zio** and so on.
correct

(kah-neh)
Don't forget **il cane!**

❏	**il metallo** *(meh-tahl-loh)*	metal	_____
❏	**il metro** *(meh-troh)*	meter	_____
❏	**milione** *(meel-yoh-neh)*	million	**m** _____
❏	**la misura** *(mee-zoo-rah)*	measure, size	_____
❏	**la moda** *(moh-dah)*	style, fashion	_____

(eem-pah-rah-reh)
Imparare!
to learn

You have already used *(doo-eh)* **due** very important verbs: *(vor-reh-ee)* **vorrei** and *(oh)* **ho**. Although you might be able
I would like I have

to get by with only these verbs, let's assume you want to do better. First,

How do you say **in italiano?**_____

How do you say **in italiano?**_____

Compare these **due** charts very carefully **e** learn these *(seh-ee)* **sei** **parole** now.
two   six

I =	*(ee-oh)* **io**	_____	we =	*(noy)* **noi**	_____
he =	*(loo-ee)* **lui**	_____	you =	*(leh-ee)* **Lei**	_____
she =	*(leh-ee)* **lei**	_____	they =	*(loh-roh)* **loro**	_____

Not too hard, is it? Draw lines between the matching **parole** *(een-gleh-zee)* **inglesi** **e** *(ee-tahl-yah-neh)* **italiane** below to

see if you can keep these **parole** straight in your mind.

(noy)
noi   I

loro   you

(leh-ee)
lei   they

Lei   he

io   we

(loo-ee)
lui   she

Note: **"Lei"** with a capital "L" means "you," and **"lei"** with a lower case "l" means "she."

❏	**il motore** *(moh-toh-reh)*	motor, engine
❏	**il momento** *(moh-men-toh)*	moment
	—**Un momento!**	Just a moment! **m**
❏	**la montagna** *(mohn-tahn-yah)*	mountain
❏	**il museo** *(moo-zeh-oh)*	museum

_____

_____

_____

_____

Adesso close **il libro e** write out both columns of this practice on a piece of **carta.** _(kar-tah)_ **paper** How did

(leh-ee) **Lei** do? _(beh-neh)_ **Bene o** _(mah-leh)_ **male? Adesso** that **Lei** know these **parole,** **Lei** can say almost anything
good **or** **bad** **you** **you**

in italiano with one basic formula: the "plug-in" formula.

To demonstrate, let's take _(seh-ee)_ **sei** basic **e** practical verbs **e** see how the "plug-in" formula works.
six

Write the verbs in the blanks after **Lei** have practiced saying them out loud many times.

(par-lah-reh)
parlare _____
to speak

(ah-bee-tah-reh)
abitare _____
to live, to reside

(or-dee-nah-reh)
ordinare _ordinare, ordinare_
to order

(kohm-prah-reh)
comprare _____
to buy

(eem-pah-rah-reh)
imparare _____
to learn

(kee-ah-mar-see)
chiamarsi _____
to be called

Besides the familiar words already circled, can **Lei** find five of the above verbs in the puzzle

below? When **Lei** find them, write them in the blanks to the right.

A	C	O	H	A	F	I	J	Y	T	P
B	O	C	E	C	H	E	A	R	E	A
I	M	P	A	R	A	R	E	L	N	R
T	P	R	E	N	D	C	O	M	E	L
A	R	M	E	C	U	E	R	E	R	A
R	A	D	U	Y	H	T	S	E	I	R
E	R	N	O	R	D	I	N	A	R	E
Y	E	G	T	S	E	D	D	O	V	E

1. _____

2. _____

3. _____

4. _____

5. _____

□ **la musica** _(moo-zee-kah)_ .... music
□ **nativo** _(nah-tee-voh)_ .... native
□ **naturale** _(nah-too-rah-leh)_ .... natural
□ **la nazione** _(nah-tsee-oh-neh)_ .... nation, country
□ **necessario** _(neh-ches-sah-ree-oh)_ .... necessary

m _____
_____

n _____
_____

Study the following patterns carefully.

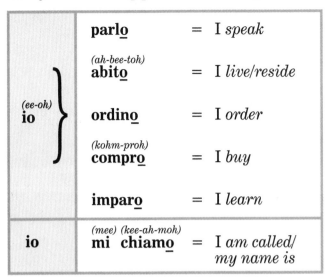

io	**parl<u>o</u>**	= I *speak*
	(ah-bee-toh) **abit<u>o</u>**	= I *live/reside*
(ee-oh)	**ordin<u>o</u>**	= I *order*
	(kohm-proh) **compr<u>o</u>**	= I *buy*
	impar<u>o</u>	= I *learn*
io	*(mee) (kee-ah-moh)* **mi chiam<u>o</u>**	= I *am called/ my name is*

noi	**parl<u>iamo</u>**	= we *speak*
	(ah-bee-tee-ah-moh) **abit<u>iamo</u>**	= we *live/reside*
(noy)	**ordin<u>iamo</u>**	= we *order*
	(kohm-pree-ah-moh) **compr<u>iamo</u>**	= we *buy*
	impar<u>iamo</u>	= we *learn*
noi	*(chee)* **ci chiam<u>iamo</u>**	= we *are called/ our name is*

Note: • With all these verbs, the first thing you do is drop the final **"are," "ere,"** or **"ire"** from the basic verb form or stem.

• With **"io,"** add **"o"** to the basic verb form.

• With **"noi,"** add **"iamo."**

(kee-ah-mar-see)
• **Chiamarsi** is a bit different, so take a few extra minutes to learn it.

Some verbs just will not conform to the pattern! But don't worry. Speak slowly **e** clearly, **e** you will be perfectly understood whether you say "**io parlo**" or "**io parla.**" Italian speakers will be delighted that you have taken the time to learn their language.

Note: • Italian has three separate ways of saying "you" whereas in English we only use one word.

• **"Lei"** will be used throughout this book and will be appropriate for most situations. **"Lei"** refers to one person in a formal sense.

(too) you
• **"Tu"** is usually reserved for family members and very close friends.

you (singular) *(voy)*
• **"Voi"** is used as the plural of both **"tu"** and **"Lei."**
you (plural)

❐	**il nome** *(noh-meh)*	name	_____
❐	**nord** *(nord)*	north	_____
❐	**normale** *(nor-mah-leh)*	normal	**n** _____
❐	**la notizia** *(noh-tee-tsee-ah)*	news, notice	_____
❐	**nuovo** *(noo-oh-voh)*	new	_____

Here's your next group of patterns.

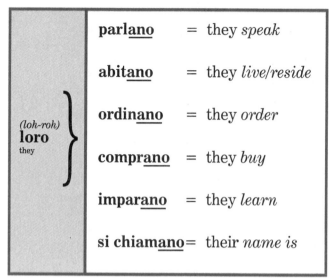

parla	= you, he, she *speak(s)*
abita	= you, he, she *live(s)/reside(s)*
(leh-ee) **Lei** you *(loo-ee)* **lui** he *(leh-ee)* **lei** she	**ordina**	= you, he, she *order(s)*
	compra	= you, he, she *buy(s)*
	impara	= you, he, she *learn(s)*
	(kee-ah-mah) **si chiama**	= your *name is* his/her *name is*

	parlano	= they *speak*
	abitano	= they *live/reside*
(loh-roh) **loro** they	**ordinano**	= they *order*
	comprano	= they *buy*
	imparano	= they *learn*
	si chiamano	= their *name is*

Note:
• Again drop the final **"are," "ere,"** or **"ire"** from the basic verb form or stem.
• With **"Lei," "lui"** and **"lei,"** add **"a"** if the original ending was **"are,"** and **"e"** for all others. (you) (she)
• With **"loro,"** simply add **"ano"** to the stem if the original ending was **"are,"** and **"ono"** for all others.

Ecco sei more verbs.
here are six

(veh-nee-reh)
venire _____
to come

(ah-veh-reh)
avere _____
to have

(dee-reh)
dire _____
to say

(ahn-dah-reh)
andare _____
to go

(ah-veh-reh) *(bee-zohn-yoh)* *(dee)*
avere bisogno di _____
to have need of

(vor-reh-ee)
vorrei _____
(I would like)

At the back of **il libro, Lei** will find twelve

(pah-jee-neh)
pagine of flash cards to help you learn these
pages

(noo-oh-veh)
parole nuove. Cut them out; carry them in
new

your briefcase, purse, pocket **o** knapsack; **e**
or

review them whenever **Lei** have a free moment.

❏	**l'occasione** *(lohk-kah-zee-oh-neh)*	occasion, opportunity	_____
❏	**occupato** *(ohk-koo-pah-toh)*	occupied, busy	_____
❏	**l'odore** *(loh-doh-reh)*	odor (smell) **o**	_____
❏	**l'oggetto** *(loh-jet-toh)*	object	_____
❏	**l'ombrello** *(lohm-brel-loh)*	umbrella	_____

Adesso, it is your turn to practice what **Lei** have learned. Fill in the following blanks with the correct form of the verb. Each time **Lei** write out the sentence, be sure to say it aloud.

(par-lah-reh)
parlare
to speak

Buon giorno!

Io _____ l'italiano. *(lee-tahl-yah-noh)*

Lei _____ l'inglese. *(leen-gleh-zeh)*
English

Lui
Lei (she) _____ il francese. *(frahn-cheh-zeh)*
French

Noi _____ il tedesco. *(teh-deh-skoh)*
German

Loro _____ lo spagnolo. *(spahn-yoh-loh)*
Spanish

(ah-bee-tah-reh)
abitare
to live, to reside

Io _____ in Italia.

Lei _____ in America.

Lui
Lei (she) _____ in Europa. *(eh-oo-roh-pah)*

Noi _____ in Inghilterra. *(een-gheel-tair-rah)*
England

Loro _____ in Francia. *(frahn-chah)*
France

(eem-pah-rah-reh)
imparare
to learn

Io _____ l'italiano.

Lei _____ lo spagnolo. *(spahn-yoh-loh)*

Lui
Lei (she) _____ il tedesco.
German

Noi _____ il francese. *(frahn-cheh-zeh)*
French

Loro _____ il cinese. *(chee-neh-zeh)*
Chinese

(or-dee-nah-reh)
ordinare
to order

Io _____ una tazza di tè. *(tah-tsah)* *(teh)*
cup

Lei _____ una tazza di caffè. *(kahf-feh)*

Lui
Lei (she) _____ un bicchiere di acqua. *(beek-kee-eh-reh)* *(ah-kwah)*
glass   water

Noi _____ due bicchieri di vino. *(beek-kee-eh-ree)*
glasses   wine

Loro _____ tre bicchieri di latte.
milk

(kohm-prah-reh)
comprare
to buy

Io _____ un libro. *(lee-broh)*

Lei _____ un' insalata. *(een-sah-lah-tah)*

Lui
Lei (she) _____ una macchina. *(mahk-kee-nah)*
car

Noi _____ otto francobolli. *(frahn-koh-bohl-lee)*
stamps

Loro _____ due birre. *(beer-reh)*
beers

(kee-ah-mar-see)
chiamarsi
to be called

Mi chiamo Elena.

Io _mi chiamo/_ _____ Nicola.

Lei _____ Giovanni.

Lui
Lei (she) _____ Martini.

Noi _____ Rizzo.

Loro _si chiamano/_ _____ Rossi.

❑ **l'opera** *(loh-peh-rah)*	opera	_____
❑ **l'ora** *(loh-rah)*	hour, time	_____
❑ **ordinario** *(or-dee-nah-ree-oh)*	ordinary	**O** _____
❑ **l'ospedale** *(loh-speh-dah-leh)*	hospital	_____
❑ **ovest** *(oh-vest)*	west	

43

Now take a break, walk around the room, take a deep breath **e** do the next **sei** verbs.

(veh-nee-reh)
venire
to come

Io _vengo/_ **dall'America.** *(dahl-lah-meh-ree-kah)*

Lei _viene/_ **dall'Inghilterra.** *(dahl-leen-gheel-tair-rah)*

Lui _____ **dal Canada.** *(kah-nah-dah)*
Lei (she)

Noi _veniamo/_ **da New York.**

Loro _vengono/_ **da Roma.** *(roh-mah)*
Rome

(ahn-dah-reh)
andare
to go

Io _vado/_ **in Italia.**

Lei _va/_ **in Francia.** *(frahn-chah)*

Lui _____ **in Spagna.** *(spahn-yah)*
Lei (she)

Noi _andiamo/_ **in Germania.** *(jair-mahn-yah)*

Loro _vanno/_ **in Portogallo.** *(por-toh-gahl-loh)*
Portugal

(vor-reh-ee)
vorrei
(I) would like

Io _____ **un bicchiere di vino.** *(beek-kee-eh-reh)* *(vee-noh)*
glass   wine

Lei _vorrebbe/_ **un bicchiere di vino rosso.** *(rohs-soh)*
red

Lui _____ **un bicchiere di vino bianco.** *(bee-ahn-koh)*
Lei (she)   white

Noi _vorremmo/_ **tre bicchieri di vino.** *(beek-kee-eh-ree)*

Loro _vorrebbero/_ **due birre.** *(beer-reh)*
beers

(dee-reh)
dire
to say

Ciao!

Io _dico/_ **"buon giorno."** *(bwohn)* *(jor-noh)*

Lei _dice/_ **"sì."**

Lui _____ **"no."**
Lei (she)

Noi _diciamo/_ **"ciao."** *(chow)*

Loro non _dicono/_ **niente.** *(nee-en-teh)*
nothing

(ah-veh-reh)
avere
to have

Io _ho/_ **venti euro.** *(ven-tee)* *(eh-oo-roh)*

Lei _ha/_ **trenta euro.** *(tren-tah)*

Lui _____ **ottanta euro.** *(oht-tahn-tah)*
Lei (she)

Noi _abbiamo/_ **cento euro.** *(chen-toh)*

Loro _hanno/_ **mille euro.** *(meel-leh)*

(ah-veh-reh) *(bee-zohn-yoh)* *(dee)*
avere bisogno di
have   need   of/to need

Io _____ **una camera.** *(kah-meh-rah)*
room

Lei _____ **un bicchiere di acqua.** *(ah-kwah)*

Lui _____ **un libro.**
Lei (she)

Noi _____ **quattro camere.** *(kah-meh-reh)*
rooms

Loro _____ **ottomila lire.**

□ **il pacco** *(pahk-koh)* . . . . package _____
□ **il paio** *(pie-yoh)* . . . . pair _____
— **un paio di scarpe** . . . . a pair of shoes **p** _____
□ **il palazzo** *(pah-lah-tsoh)* . . . . palace, building _____
44 □ **i pantaloni** *(pahn-tah-loh-nee)* . . . . pants, trousers _____

Sì, it is hard to get used to all those **parole nuove.** Just keep practicing **e** before **Lei** know

it, **Lei** will be using them naturally. **Adesso** is a perfect time to turn to the back of this **libro,**

clip out your verb flash cards **e** start flashing. Don't skip over your free **parole** either. Check

them off in the box provided as **Lei impara** *(eem-pah-rah)* each one. See if **Lei** can fill in the blanks

below. **Le risposte corrette** are at the bottom of **la pagina.** *page*

1. _____

    (I speak Italian.)

2. _____

    (We learn Italian.)

3. _____

    (She needs 500 euro.)

4. _____

    (He comes from the United States.)

5. _____

    (They live in Canada.)

6. _____

    (You buy a book.)

In the following Steps, **Lei** will be introduced to more verbs **e Lei** should drill them in exactly the same way as **Lei** did in this section. Look up **le parole nuove** in your **dizionario** *(dee-tsee-oh-nah-ree-oh)* **e** make up your own *dictionary* sentences. Try out your **parole nuove** for that's how you make them yours to use on your holiday. Remember, the more **Lei** practice **adesso,** the more enjoyable your trip will be. **Buona fortuna!** *(bwoh-nah)* *(for-too-nah)* *good* *luck*

LE RISPOSTE

1. **Io parlo l'italiano.**
2. **Noi impariamo l'italiano.**
3. **Lei ha bisogno di cinquecento euro.**
4. **Lui viene dagli Stati Uniti.**
5. **Loro abitano in Canada.**
6. **Lei compra un libro.**

45

(keh) *(oh-rah)* *(eh)*
Che ora è?
what   time   is it

(jor-nee)
Lei know how to tell **i giorni della settimana e i mesi dell' anno,** so now let's learn to tell
days   week   months   year

(meh-zee) (del-lah-noh)

time. As a traveler **in Italia, Lei** need to be able to tell time in order to make *(preh-noh-tah-tsee-oh-nee)* **prenotazioni**
reservations

(ahp-poon-tah-men-tee)   *(treh-nee)*
e appuntamenti, e to catch **treni e autobus. Ecco** the "basics."
appointments   trains   buses   here are

What time is it?	=	**Che ora è?** *(keh) (oh-rah) (eh)*
noon	=	**mezzogiorno** *(med-zoh-jor-noh)*
midnight	=	**mezzanotte** *(med-zah-noht-teh)*
half past	=	**e mezzo** *(med-zoh)*
minus	=	**meno** *(meh-noh)*
a quarter	=	**un quarto** *(kwar-toh)*
a quarter to/before	=	**meno un quarto** *(meh-noh)*
a quarter after/past	=	**e un quarto** *(eh) (kwar-toh)*

Adesso quiz yourself. Fill in the missing letters below.

midnight = `m` `e` `☐` `☐` `a` `n` `o` `☐` `☐` `e`   minus = `m` `e` `☐` `☐`

quarter before = `m` `e` `n` `✕` `n` `✕` `☐` `a` `r` `t` `o`

half past = `☐` `✕` `m` `e` `☐` `☐` `o` and finally

What time is it? `C` `h` `☐` `✕` `o` `r` `☐` `✕` `☐` `?`

Adesso, come are these **parole** used? Study **gli** **esempi** below. When **Lei** think it through, it
(l-yee) (eh-zem-pee)
how *examples*

really is not too difficult. Just notice that the pattern changes after the halfway mark. Notice

that the phrase "o'clock" is not used in Italian.

Sono le cinque.
(cheen-kweh)
it is *five o'clock*

`5,00`   *Sono le cinque. Sono le cinque.*

Sono le cinque e dieci.
(dee-eh-chee)

`5,10`   _____

Sono le cinque e un quarto.
(kwar-toh)
and a *quarter*

`5,15`   _____

Sono le cinque e venti.
(ven-tee)

`5,20`   _____

Sono le cinque e mezzo.
(med-zoh)
half past five

`5,30`   _____

Sono le sei meno venti.
(seh-ee)(meh-noh)

`5,40`   _____

Sono le sei meno un quarto.

`5,45`   _____

Sono le sei meno dieci.

`5,50`   _____

Sono le sei.
(seh-ee)

`6,00`   _____

See how **importante** learning **i numeri** is? Answer the following **domande** based on **gli**
(eem-por-tahn-teh) *(noo-meh-ree)* *(doh-mahn-deh)* *(l-yee)*
questions

orologi below.
(oh-roh-loh-jee)
clocks

1. `8,00` _____

2. `7,15` _____

3. `4,30` _____

4. `9,20` _____

47

When **Lei** answer a "**quando?**" *(kwahn-doh)* question, say "**alle**" *(ahl-leh)* before **Lei** give the time.

when / at

1. **Quando** *(kwahn-doh)* **viene** *(vee-eh-neh)* **il treno?** *(treh-noh)* _____ *alle sei*
   comes / train — (at 6,00)

2. **Quando viene l'autobus?** *(lah-oo-toh-boos)* _____
   comes / bus — (at 7,30)

3. **Quando comincia** *(koh-meen-chah)* **il concerto?** *(kohn-chair-toh)* _____
   begins/commences / concert — (at 8,00)

4. **Quando comincia il film?** *(feelm)* _____
   begins / film — (at 9,00)

5. **Quando è aperto** *(ah-pair-toh)* **il ristorante?** *(ree-stoh-rahn-teh)* _____
   is / open — (at 11,30)

6. **Quando è aperta** *(ah-pair-tah)* **la banca?** *(bahn-kah)* _____
   open — (at 8,30)

7. **Quando è chiuso** *(kee-oo-zoh)* **il ristorante?** _____
   closed — (at 5,30)

8. **Quando è chiusa** *(kee-oo-zah)* **la banca?** _____
   — (at 10,30)

Ecco a quick quiz. Fill in the blanks **con** *(kohn)* the correct **numeri.**

here is / with

9. **Un minuto** *(mee-noo-toh)* **ha** *(ah)* _____ **secondi.** *(seh-kohn-dee)*
   minute / has / (?) / seconds

10. **Un'ora** *(oo-noh-rah)* **ha** *(ah)* _____ **minuti.**
   hour / has / (?) / minutes

11. **Una settimana** *(oo-nah)* **ha** *(ah)* _____ **giorni.** *(jor-nee)*
   week / (?) / days

12. **Un anno** *(ahn-noh)* **ha** *(ah)* _____ **mesi.** *(meh-zee)*
   year / has / (?) / months

13. **Un anno ha** _____ **settimane.** *(set-tee-mah-neh)*
   (?) / weeks

14. **Un anno ha** _____ **giorni.** *(jor-nee)*
   (?)

Do **Lei** remember your greetings from earlier? It is a good time to review them as they will

always be *(mohl-toh)* **molto** **importanti.**
very   important

(ah-leh) *(dee)* *(see)(dee-cheh)* *(jor-noh)* *(seen-yoh-rah)*
Alle otto di mattina, si dice, "Buon giorno, signora Fellini."
at   in the morning   one says   good   morning

(dee-chah-moh)
Che diciamo?_____ Buon giorno, signora Fellini. _____
what   do we say

(ah-loo-nah) *(poh-meh-ree-joh)* *(seen-yor)* *(frahn-kee)*
All'una del pomeriggio, si dice, "Buon giorno, signor Franchi."
one   afternoon   Mr.

Che diciamo? _____

(seh-rah) *(seen-yoh-ree-nah)*
Alle otto di sera, si dice, "Buona sera, signorina Rizzo."
evening   Miss

(keh)
Che diciamo? _____

(see) *(bwoh-nah) (noht-teh)*
Alle dieci di sera, si dice, "Buona notte."
ten   good   night

Che diciamo? _____

Lei have probably already noticed that plurals are *generally* formed in the following way.

(bee-chee-klet-tah)	*(bee-chee-klet-teh)*
la bicicletta	**le biciclette**
bicycle	bicycles
(loh-rah)	*(oh-reh)*
l' ora	**le ore**
hour	hours
(kah-neh)	*(kah-nee)*
il cane	**i cani**
dog	dogs
(gaht-toh)	*(gaht-tee)*
il gatto	**i gatti**
cat	cats

In italiano adjectives agree with the gender and number of the nouns they modify **e** they

generally come after the noun (but not always!)

(rohs-sah)	*(rohs-seh)*
la bicicletta rossa	**le biciclette rosse**
red	
(neh-roh)	*(neh-ree)*
il telefono nero	**i telefoni neri**
black	

❏	**la partenza** *(par-ten-tsah)*	departure	**p** _____
❏	**il passaporto** *(pahs-sah-por-toh)*	passport	_____
❏	**la pasta** *(pah-stah)*	pasta (**fettucine, ravioli,** etc.) _____
❏	**la patata** *(pah-tah-tah)*	potato	_____
❏	**la penna** *(pen-nah)*	pen	

Ecco due verbi nuovi per *(pair)* **Step 13.**

(mahn-jah-reh)
mangiare _____
to eat

(beh-reh)
bere _____
to drink

(mahn-jah-reh)
mangiare
to eat

(beh-reh)
bere
to drink

Io _mangio/_ _____ *(leen-sah-lah-tah)* **l'insalata.**

Lei _____ **la** *(mee-neh-strah)* **minestra.**
soup

Lui _____ **molto.**
Lei (she)   a lot

Noi _____ *(pah-neh)* **il pane.**
bread

Loro non _____ *(nee-en-teh)* **niente.**
nothing

Io _____ *(laht-teh)* **il latte.**
milk

Lei non _____ *(nee-en-teh)* **niente.**
nothing

Lui _beve/_ _____ **il tè.**
Lei (she)

Noi _____ **il caffè.**

Loro _____ **il vino bianco.**

Lei have learned that to negate a statement, simply add **non** before the verb. Notice in the

examples above, that when you use the word "**niente**," you also need to add "**non**" before the verb.

nothing

(dee-koh) (nee-en-teh)
Io non dico niente.
I   say   nothing

Noi non compriamo niente.
we   buy   nothing

OR

Non dico niente.

Non compriamo niente.

- ☐ **perfetto** *(pair-fet-toh)* . . . . perfect
- ☐ **il periodo** *(peh-ree-oh-doh)* . . . . period
- ☐ **la permanenza** *(pair-mah-nen-tsah)* . . . . stay, permanence
- ☐ **il permesso** *(pair-mes-soh)* . . . . permission
-    **— Permesso?** . . . . May I come in?

p _____

Lei have learned a lot of material in the last few steps **e** that means it is time to quiz yourself. Don't panic, this is just for you **e** no one else needs to know how **Lei** did. Remember, this is a chance to review, find out what **Lei** remember **e** what **Lei** need to spend more time on. After **Lei** have finished, check your **risposte** in the glossary at the back of this book. Circle the correct answers.

il caffè	tea	coffee
no	yes	no
la zia	aunt	uncle
o	and	or
imparare	to drink	to learn
mattina	morning	night
martedì	Friday	Tuesday
parlare	to live	to speak
(leh-stah-teh) **l'estate**	summer	winter
il denaro	money	page
dieci	nine	ten
molto	a lot	bread

la famiglia	seven	family
i figli	children	grandfather
il latte	butter	~~milk~~
il sale	pepper	salt
sotto	under	over
il medico	man	doctor
giugno	June	July
la cucina	kitchen	religions
(oh) **ho**	I need	I have
ordinare	to order	to buy
(ee-eh-ree) **ieri**	yesterday	tomorrow
(jahl-loh) **giallo**	good	yellow

(koh-meh) (vah)
Come va? <u>What time is it?</u> <u>How are you?</u> Well, how are you after this quiz?

☐	**la persona** *(pair-soh-nah)*	person	_____
☐	**il pezzo** *(peh-tsoh)*	piece	_____
☐	**il piacere** *(pee-ah-cheh-reh)*	pleasure **p**	_____
	— **per piacere**	if you please	_____
	— **Molto piacere**	"It's a pleasure to meet you."	_____

14   *(nord)* *(sood)* *(est)* *(oh-vest)*
Nord - Sud, Est - Ovest
north   south   east   west

If **Lei** are looking at **una** *(kar-tah) (jeh-oh-grah-fee-kah)* **carta geografica** **e Lei** see the following **parole,** it should not be too map

difficult to figure out what they mean. Take an educated guess.

(lah-meh-ree-kah)
l'America del nord

(lah-meh-ree-kah) *(sood)*
l'America del sud

il Polo nord

il Polo sud

(dah-koh-tah)
il Dakota del nord

(kah-roo-lee-nah)
la Carolina del sud

(leer-lahn-dah)
l'Irlanda del nord

(sood-ah-free-kah)
il Sudafrica

(pair)
Le parole italiane per "north," "south," "east" **e** "west" are easy to recognize due to their

similitudini to **inglese.** These **parole sono molto importanti.** Learn them **oggi!** *(oh-jee)*
are

(nord)
nord _____
north

(oh-vest)
ovest _____
west

(est)
est _____
east

(sood)
sud_____
south

(see-nee-strah)
sinistra

(dee-reet-toh)
diritto

(deh-strah)
destra

_____   _____   _____
(left)   (straight ahead)   (right)

LE RISPOSTE

South Africa	Northern Ireland
South Carolina	North Dakota
South Pole	North Pole
South America	North America

These **parole** can go a long way. Say them aloud each time you write them in the blanks below.

(pair) (fah-voh-reh)
per favore _____
please

(grah-tsee-eh)
grazie _____
thank you

(mee) (skoo-zee)
me scusi _____
excuse me

(preh-goh)
prego _____
you're welcome

(kohn-vair-sah-tsee-oh-nee) *(tee-pee-keh) (pair)*
Ecco due conversazioni   very **tipiche per** someone who is trying to find something.
two   conversations   typical   for

Write them out in the blanks below.

Gianni: **Mi scusi. Dov'è l'Albergo Florio?**
              excuse me   *(lahl-bair-goh)*

_____ *Mi scusi. Dov'è l'Albergo Florio?* _____

(kohn-tee-noo-ee) (dee-reet-toh) (poy) (jee-ree)   (strah-dah)
Pietro: **Continui   diritto, poi giri a sinistra alla seconda strada.**
              straight ahead   then   turn   street

_____

(lee)
L'Albergo Florio è lì a destra.
              there   to the right

_____

(veel-lah) (joo-lee-ah)
Stefano: **Mi scusi. Dov'è la Villa Giulia?**

_____

(jee-ree) (kwee)   (kohn-tee-noo-ee)   (pair) (chen-toh)(meh-tree)
Andrea: **Giri qui a destra. Continui   diritto per cento metri.**
              turn   here   meters

_____

(poy)   *(ahl-lahn-goh-loh)*
Poi giri a sinistra e la Villa Giulia è all'angolo.
then   at the corner

_____

❐	**il piatto** *(pee-aht-toh)*	plate, dish	_____
❐	**la piazza** *(pee-ah-tsah)*	plaza, town square	_____
❐	**la pillola** *(peel-loh-lah)*	pill	_____
❐	**pittoresco** *(peet-toh-reh-skoh)*	picturesque **p**	_____
❐	**la polizia** *(poh-lee-tsee-ah)*	police	_____

Are **Lei** lost? There is no need to be lost if **Lei ha** ^(ah) learned the basic **parole di direzione.** ^(dee-reh-tsee-oh-neh)

Do not try to memorize these **conversazioni** because **Lei** will never be looking for precisely these places. One day, **Lei** might need to ask **direzioni** to "il **Foro Romano**" ^{(foh-roh)(roh-mah-noh)} or "il **Colosseo.**" ^(koh-lohs-seh-oh) Learn the key direction **parole e** be sure **Lei** can find your **destinazione.** ^(deh-stee-nah-tsee-oh-neh) **Lei** may want to buy a guidebook to start planning which places **Lei** would like to visit. Practice asking **direzioni** to these special places. What if the person responding to your **domanda** answers too quickly for **Lei** to understand the entire reply? Practice saying,

Mi scusi. Io non capisco. Ripeta, per favore!

(kah-pee-skoh) *(ree-peh-tah)* *(pair)*

I   do not   understand   repeat

Adesso, say it again **e** then write it out below.

_____

(Excuse me. I do not understand. Please repeat.)

Sì, è difficile ^(see) at first but don't give up! **Quando** the directions are repeated, **Lei** will be able to

yes   difficult   when

understand if **Lei ha** ^(ah) learned the key **parole.** Let's review by writing them in the blanks below.

have

right

_____
(north)

_____
(west)

_____
(east)

left

_____
(south)

☐	**la porta** *(por-tah)*	door	_____
☐	**il porto** *(por-toh)*	port	_____
☐	**la porzione** *(por-tsee-oh-neh)*	portion	_____
☐	**possibile** *(pohs-see-bee-leh)*	possible	_____
☐	**la posta** *(poh-stah)*	post office, mail	_____

p

Ecco quattro verbi nuovi.
(noo-oh-vee)
verbs   new

(troh-vah-reh)
trovare _____
to find

(kah-pee-reh)
capire _____
to understand

(ven-deh-reh)
vendere _____
to sell

(ree-peh-teh-reh)
ripetere _____
to repeat

As always, say each sentence out loud. Say each **e** every **parola** carefully, pronouncing each

Italian sound as well as **Lei** can.

(troh-vah-reh)
trovare
to find

Io _____ **l'albergo.**
(lahl-bair-goh)

Lei _____ **la gondola.**
(gohn-doh-lah)
Venetian boat

Lui _____ **la banca.**
Lei (she)

Noi _____ **il museo.**

Loro _____ **il denaro.**
money

(kah-pee-reh)
capire
to understand

Io *capisco/* _____ **l'italiano.**
(lee-tahl-yah-noh)

Lei *capisce/* _____ **l'inglese.**
(leen-gleh-zeh)

Lui _____ **il tedesco.**
Lei (she)
(teh-deh-skoh)
German

Noi *capiamo/* _____ **il russo.**
(roos-soh)
Russian

Loro *capiscono/* _____ **il francese.**
(frahn-cheh-zeh)
French

(ven-deh-reh)
vendere
to sell

Io _____ **dei fiori.**
(deh-ee)

Lei _____ **della frutta.**
(del-lah)

Lui _____ **dei libri.**
Lei (she)

Noi _____ **dei biglietti.**
(beel-yet-tee)

Loro _____ **dei francobolli.**
(frahn-koh-bohl-lee)
stamps

(ree-peh-teh-reh)
ripetere
to repeat

Che? Che? Che?

Io _____ **la parola.**

Lei _____ **la risposta.**
(ree-spoh-stah)
answer

Lui _____ **la lezione.**
Lei (she)
(leh-tsee-oh-neh)
lesson

Noi _____ **i nomi.**
(noh-mee)
names

Loro _____ **le direzioni.**
(dee-reh-tsee-oh-nee)
directions

❑	**povero** *(poh-veh-roh)*	poor
❑	**precedente** *(preh-cheh-den-teh)*	preceding
❑	**preciso** *(preh-chee-zoh)*	precise, exact
	— **alle sei preciso**	at six o'clock on the dot
❑	**presente** *(preh-zen-teh)*	present

p

_____
_____
_____
_____
_____

(dee) (soh-prah) (dee) (soht-toh)
Di Sopra – Di Sotto
above/upstairs   below/downstairs

(ahn-koh-rah)   *(kah-meh-rah)*
Adesso impariamo ancora delle parole. Ecco una casa in Italia. Go to your **camera da**
(we) learn   more   bedroom

letto e look around. Let's learn **i nomi delle cose nella camera** just like we learned the
of the   things   in the

various parts of **la casa.**

(kah-meh-rah) (let-toh) (soh-prah)
La camera da letto è di sopra.
bedroom   upstairs

(lar-mah-dee-oh)
l' armadio _____
wardrobe

(let-toh)
il letto _____
bed

(koo-shee-noh)
il cuscino _____
pillow

(koh-pair-tah)
la coperta _____
blanket

(zvel-yah)
la sveglia _____
alarm clock

(sah-loht-toh) (soht-toh)
Il salotto è di sotto.
living room   downstairs

_____ è la camera da letto?
(where)   (where)

❐ **prezioso** *(preh-tsee-oh-zoh)* .... precious, valuable _____
❐ **il prezzo** *(preh-tsoh)* .... price _____
❐ **il problema** *(proh-bleh-mah)* .... problem   **p** _____
❐ **pronto** *(prohn-toh)* .... prompt, ready _____
  — **"Pronto!"** .... "Hello!" (answering telephone) _____

Adesso, remove the next **cinque** stickers **e** label these **cose nella** *(soo-ah)* **Sua** camera da letto. Let's

your

move **nella Sua stanza da** *(bahn-yoh)* **bagno e** do the same thing. Remember, **la stanza da bagno** means

into   your   bathroom

a room to bathe in. If **Lei è in un ristorante e Lei** *(ah) (bee-zohn-yoh)* **ha bisogno** del lavatory, **Lei** want to ask for

need

(gah-bee-net-tee) **i gabinetti e** *not* for **la stanza da bagno.** Restrooms may be marked with pictures **o**

or

simply **"signore" e "signori."** Don't confuse them!

(seen-yoh-reh)
SIGNORE
ladies

(seen-yoh-ree)
SIGNORI
men

(ahn-keh)
La stanza da bagno è anche di sopra.
bathroom   also

(spek-kee-oh)
lo specchio _____
mirror

(lah-vahn-dee-noh)
il lavandino _____
washstand

(l-yee) (ah-shoo-gah-mah-nee)
gli asciugamani _____
towels

(vee-chee)
il W.C. _____
toilet

(doh-chah)
la doccia _____
shower

(loof-fee-choh) (ahn-keh)
L'ufficio è anche di sotto.
study   also   downstairs

❏ **la qualifica** *(kwah-lee-fee-kah)*	qualification	_____
❏ **la qualità** *(kwah-lee-tah)*	quality	_____
❏ **la quantità** *(kwahn-tee-tah)*	quantity **q**	_____
❏ **il quartiere** *(kwar-tee-eh-reh)*	quarter, district	_____
❏ **quarto** *(kwar-toh)*	quarter, fourth	_____

Non forget to remove the next group of stickers **e** label these things in your **stanza da bagno.**

Okay, it is time to review. Here's a quick quiz to see what you remember.

ladies

men

downstairs

please

towels

upstairs

bathroom

lavatory/restroom

straight ahead

I understand

di sotto

(seen-yoh-ree)
signori

(pair)
per favore

(kah-pee-skoh)
io capisco

(gah-bee-net-tee)
i gabinetti

(dee-reet-toh)
diritto

(l-yee) (ah-shoo-gah-mah-nee)
gli asciugamani

(seen-yoh-reh)
signore

di sopra

(bahn-yoh)
la stanza da bagno

☐	**la radio** *(rah-dee-oh)*	radio	
☐	**la ragione** *(rah-joh-neh)*	reason	
☐	**rapido** *(rah-pee-doh)*	rapid, fast	**r**
☐	**recente** *(reh-chen-teh)*	recent	
☐	**il resto** *(reh-stoh)*	rest, change (money)	

Next stop — **l'ufficio,** *(loof-fee-choh)* specifically **il tavolo** *(tah-voh-loh)* o **la scrivania** *(skree-vah-nee-ah)* **nell'ufficio.** *(nel-loof-fee-choh)* **Che** *(keh)* **c'è** *(cheh)* **sulla** *(sool-lah)*
office   table   desk   is there   on the

scrivania? Let's identify **le cose** which one normally finds **sulla scrivania** or strewn about
                                things

l'ufficio. *(loof-fee-choh)*

il televisore *(teh-leh-vee-zoh-reh)*
television

la matita *(mah-tee-tah)*
pencil

la penna *(pen-nah)*
pen

il computer *(kohm-pyoo-tair)*
computer

la carta *(kar-tah)*
paper

il cestino *(cheh-stee-noh)*
basket

il giornale *(jor-nah-leh)*
newspaper

il giornale

la rivista *(ree-vee-stah)*
magazine

gli occhiali *(l-yee) (ohk-kee-ah-lee)*
eyeglasses

il libro *(lee-broh)*
book

☐ **ricco** *(reek-koh)*	rich	
☐ **la ricetta** *(ree-chet-tah)*	recipe	
☐ **il ricordo** *(ree-kor-doh)*	souvenir, record	**r**
☐ **il Rinascimento** *(ree-nah-shee-men-toh)* . . .	Renaissance	
☐ **il rispetto** *(ree-spet-toh)*	respect	

Don't forget these essentials!

(let-teh-rah)
la lettera
letter

(frahn-koh-bohl-loh)
il francobollo
stamp

(kar-toh-lee-nah)
la cartolina
postcard

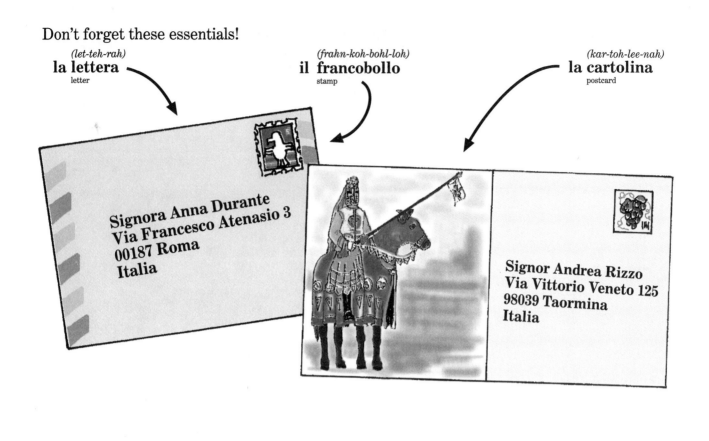

| _____ | _____ | _____ |
| (letter) | (stamp) | (postcard) |

The expressions **"vero"** *(veh-roh)* o **"non è vero"** are useful **in italiano.** When added to the end of a sentence, the sentence becomes a question for which **la risposta** is usually **"sì."** *(see)* Compare them to their equivalents **in inglese.**
yes

Lei è italiano, vero?
You are Italian, aren't you?

Sofia è bella, non è vero?
Sophia is beautiful, isn't she?

È un libro, vero?
It's a book, isn't it?

Remember if you add <u>**non**</u> before a verb **Lei** negate the sentence.
not

Io vorrei un bicchiere di acqua.
I would like *(beek-kee-eh-reh)* glass *(ah-kwah)* water

Io non vorrei un bicchiere di acqua.
would not like *(vor-reh-ee)* water

In italiano, if you wish, you may drop the subject of the sentence.

(kah-pee-skoh) (lee-tahl-yah-noh)
Io capisco l'italiano.
understand

(veh-nee-ah-moh)(dahl-yee)
Noi veniamo dagli Stati Uniti.
come from

OR

Capisco l'italiano.

Veniamo dagli Stati Uniti.

☐	**il ristorante** *(ree-stoh-rahn-teh)*	restaurant	_____
☐	**ritardo** *(ree-tar-doh)*.....................	late	_____
☐	**la rivista** *(ree-vee-stah)*	magazine, review **r**	_____
☐	**Roma** *(roh-mah)*........................	Rome	_____
☐	**la rosa** *(roh-zah)*	rose	_____

60

Simple, isn't it? **Adesso**, after you fill in the blanks below, go back a second time and negate all these sentences by adding **"non"** before each verb. Then go back a third time **e** drop the subject. Don't get discouraged! Just look at how much **Lei** have already learned **e** think ahead to *(tor-reh) (pen-den-teh)* **pasta, la Torre Pendente e** new adventures.
Leaning Tower

(veh-deh-reh)
vedere _____
to see

(mahn-dah-reh)
mandare _____
to send

(dor-mee-reh)
dormire _____
to sleep

(fah-reh)
fare _____
to do, to make

(veh-deh-reh)
vedere
to see

Io _____ il **mercato.** *(mair-kah-toh)*

Lei _vedel_____ il **Museo Borghese.**

Lui _____ il **Colosseo.** *(koh-lohs-seh-oh)*
Lei (she) Colosseum

Noi _____ il **Mare Mediterraneo.**
Mediterranean Sea

Loro _____ le **montagne.** *(mohn-tahn-yeh)*
mountains

(mahn-dah-reh)
mandare
to send

Io _____ la **lettera.** *(let-teh-rah)*
letter

Lei _____ la **cartolina.**

Lui _mandal_____ il **libro.**
Lei (she)

Noi _____ due **cartoline.** *(kar-toh-lee-neh)*
postcards

Loro _____ tre **lettere.**

(dor-mee-reh)
dormire
to sleep

Io _____ nella **camera.** *(kah-meh-rah)*

Lei _____ nell'**albergo.**

Lui _dormel_____ nella **casa.**
Lei (she)

Noi _____ sotto la **coperta.** *(koh-pair-tah)*
under blanket

Loro _____ senza i **cuscini.** *(sen-zah) (koo-shee-nee)*
without pillows

(fah-reh)
fare
to do, to make

Io _facciol_____ **tutto.** *(toot-toh)*
everything

Lei _fal_____ una **telefonata.** *(teh-leh-foh-nah-tah)*
telephone call

Lui _____ **molto.** *(mohl-toh)*
Lei (she) a lot

Noi non _facciamol_____ **niente.** *(nee-en-teh)*
nothing

Loro _fannol_____ **tutto.** *(toot-toh)*
everything

☐ **il sacco** *(sahk-koh)* .... sack, bag
☐ **il sale** *(sah-leh)* .... salt **S** _____
— **Sali e Tabacchi** .... salt and tobacco store _____
☐ **la salsa** *(sahl-sah)* .... sauce _____
☐ **il saluto** *(sah-loo-toh)* .... greeting, salutation _____

Before **Lei** proceed with the next step, **per favore** identify all the items **qui sotto.**
(kwee) here

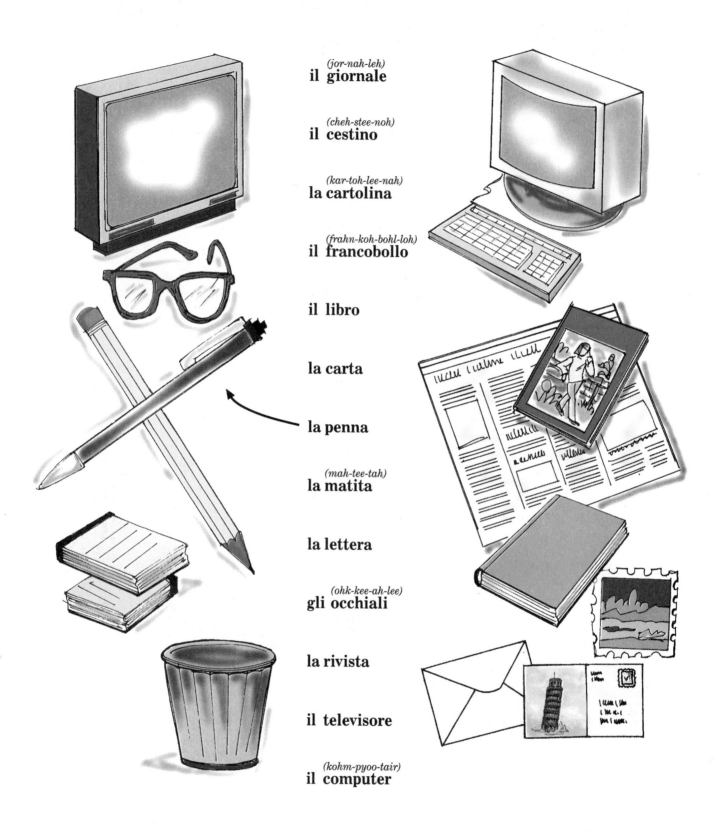

(jor-nah-leh)
il **giornale**

(cheh-stee-noh)
il **cestino**

(kar-toh-lee-nah)
la **cartolina**

(frahn-koh-bohl-loh)
il **francobollo**

il **libro**

la **carta**

la **penna**

(mah-tee-tah)
la **matita**

la **lettera**

(ohk-kee-ah-lee)
gli **occhiali**

la **rivista**

il **televisore**

(kohm-pyoo-tair)
il **computer**

❏ **la scala** *(skah-lah)*	staircase, stairs	_____
— **la Scala**	opera house in Milan	_____
❏ **lo scavo** *(skah-voh)*	excavation	_____
❏ **la scena** *(sheh-nah)*	scene **S**	_____
❏ **la scienza** *(shee-en-zah)*	science	_____

Adesso Lei *(leh-ee)* know how to count, how to ask **domande,** how to use **verbi con** the "plug-in"
questions

formula **e** how to describe something, be it the location of **un albergo o il colore di una casa.**
house

Let's take the basics that **Lei ha** learned **e** expand them in special areas that will be most helpful

in your travels. What does everyone do on a holiday? Send postcards, **non è vero?** *(veh-roh)* Let's
don't they

learn exactly how **l'ufficio postale** *(poh-stah-leh)* **italiano** works.
post office

la posta *(poh-stah)*
mail

in Spagna *(spahn-yah)*
to

in Inghilterra *(een-gheel-tair-rah)*

in Francia *(frahn-chah)*

in America *(ah-meh-ree-kah)*

The **PT (Poste e Telecomunicazioni)** *(pee-tee) (poh-steh) (teh-leh-koh-moo-nee-kah-tsee-oh-nee)* is where **Lei** buy **francobolli,** send **pacchi,** *(pahk-kee)*
post office   packages

cartoline e lettere. Lei may also buy **francobolli** at the local **tabaccheria** *(tah-bahk-keh-ree-ah)* of which there are
tobacco shop

many. If **Lei ha bisogno** *(bee-zohn-yoh)* to call home **in America,** this can also be done at the **PT. Le PT** *(pee-tee)*

sono closed on Sunday.

❏ **secondo** *(seh-kohn-doh)*	second	_____
❏ **il segnale** *(sen-yah-leh)*	signal, sign	_____
❏ **il segretario** *(seh-greh-tah-ree-oh)*	secretary (male) **S**	_____
❏ **la selezione** *(seh-leh-tsee-oh-neh)*	selection, choice	_____
❏ **la semisfera** *(seh-mee-sfeh-rah)*	hemisphere	_____

Ecco some **parole necessarie** *(neh-ches-sah-ree-eh)* **per l'ufficio postale.** Practice them aloud **e** then write them in the blanks.

(let-teh-rah)
la lettera
letter

(kar-toh-lee-nah)
la cartolina
postcard

_____

_____

(pahk-koh)
il pacco
package

(teh-leh-grahm-mah)
il telegramma
telegram

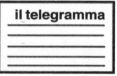

_____

_____

(vee-ah) (ah-eh-reh-ah)
via aerea
by airmail

(fahx)
il fax

_____

_____

(frahn-koh-bohl-loh)
il francobollo
stamp

(kah-bee-nah)(teh-leh-foh-nee-kah)
la cabina telefonica
telephone booth

_____

_____

(boo-kah) (del-leh) (let-teh-reh)
la buca delle lettere
mailbox

(teh-leh-foh-noh)
il telefono

_____

_____

☐ **semplice** *(sem-plee-cheh)*	simple, easy		_____
☐ **il sentimento** *(sen-tee-men-toh)*	feeling		_____
☐ **serio** *(seh-ree-oh)*	serious	**S**	_____
☐ **il servizio** *(sair-vee-tsee-oh)*	service		_____
☐ **sfortunato** *(sfor-too-nah-toh)*	unfortunate, unlucky		_____

64

Next step — **Lei** ask **domande** like those **sotto,** depending on what **Lei vorrebbe.** Repeat
questions
(vor-reb-beh)
would like

these sentences aloud many times.

Dove compro i francobolli?_____
do I buy

Dove compro una cartolina?_____

(fah-choh) *(teh-leh-foh-nah-tah)* *(een-tair-oor-bah-nah)*
Dove faccio una telefonata interurbana? _____
do I make telephone call long-distance

(boo-kah) *(let-teh-reh)*
Dov'è la buca delle lettere? _____
where is mailbox

(teh-leh-foh-nee-kah)
Dov'è la cabina telefonica?_____
telephone booth

(mahn-doh) *(pahk-koh)*
Dove mando un pacco? _____
do I send

(fah-choh)
Dove faccio una telefonata?_____
do I make telephone call

Quanto costa?_____ *Quanto costa? Quanto costa?* _____
how much

Adesso, quiz yourself. See if **Lei** can translate the following thoughts **in italiano.**

1. Where is the telephone booth? _____

2. Where do I make a telephone call? _____

3. Where do I make a long-distance telephone call? _____

4. Where is the post office? _____

5. Where do I buy stamps? _____

6. Airmail stamps? _____

7. Where do I send a package? _____

8. Where do I send a fax? _____

65

Ecco quattro verbi nuovi.
verbs

(ah-spet-tah-reh)
aspettare _____
to wait (for)

(mee) (dee-ah)
mi dia . . . _____
give me

(skree-veh-reh)
scrivere _____
to write

(pah-gah-reh)
pagare _____
to pay (for)

Practice these verbs by not only filling in the blanks, but by saying them aloud many, many times until you are comfortable with the sounds **e** the words.

(ah-spet-tah-reh)
aspettare
to wait (for)

Io _aspetto/_ *(treh-noh)* il **treno.**

Lei _____ *(lah-oo-toh-boos)* l'**autobus.**

Lui _____ *(tahs-see)* il **tassì.**
Lei (she)   taxi

Noi _____ *(nel-lahl-bair-goh)* **nell'albergo.**
                                                    hotel

Loro _____ **davanti all'albergo.**

(skree-veh-reh)
scrivere
to write

Io _____ *(leen-dee-ree-tsoh)* l'**indirizzo.**
                                            address

Lei _scrive/_ **molto.**
              a lot

Lui non _____ *(nee-en-teh)* **niente.**
Lei (she)   nothing

Noi _____ *(doo-eh)* **due lettere.**

Loro _____ *(noh-mee)* i **loro nomi.**
                          their   names

(mee) (dee-ah)
mi dia . . .
give me

Mi _dia/_ *(kohn-toh)(pair)* il **conto, per favore.**
            bill

_____ *(meh-noo)* il **menù, per favore.**

_____ *(beel-yet-toh)* il **biglietto, per favore.**

_____ *(leen-dee-ree-tsoh)* l'**indirizzo, per favore.**
                    address

_____ *(noh-meh)* il **nome, per favore.**
                              name

(pah-gah-reh)
pagare
to pay (for)

Io _pago/_ *(kohn-toh)* il **conto.**
            bill

Lei _paga/_ *(tahs-sah)* la **tassa.**
            tax

Lui _____ *(preh-tsoh)* il **prezzo.**
Lei (she)   price

Noi _paghiamo/_ *(toot-toh)* **tutto.**
                              everything

Loro non _pagano/_ *(noh-mee)* **niente.**
                                nothing

❑ **sicuro** *(see-koo-roh)* . . . . sure, safe, secure _____
❑ **il sidro** *(see-droh)* . . . . cider _____
❑ **la sigaretta** *(see-gah-ret-tah)* . . . . cigarette **S** _____
❑ **il sigaro** *(see-gah-roh)* . . . . cigar _____
❑ **simile** *(see-mee-leh)* . . . . similar _____

Some of these signs you probably recognize, but take a couple of minutes to review them anyway.

(proh-ee-bee-toh) (lah-ches-soh)
proibito   l'accesso
road closed to vehicles

(doh-gah-nah)
dogana
customs

(vee-eh-tah-toh) (lah-ches-soh)
vietato   l'accesso
no entrance

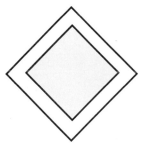

(strah-dah)
strada principale
main road, you have the right of way

(cheh-deh-reh) (eel) (pahs-soh)
cedere   il   passo
yield

(lee-mee-teh) (dee) (veh-loh-chee-tah)
limite   di velocità
speed limit

(dee-vee-eh-toh)   (soh-stah)
divieto   di sosta
no parking

(dee-vee-eh-toh)   (sor-pahs-soh)
divieto   di sorpasso
no passing

(ahlt)
alt
stop

(deh-vee-ah-tsee-oh-neh)
DEVIAZIONE
detour

What follows are approximate conversions, so when you order something by liters, kilograms or grams you will have an idea of what to expect and not find yourself being handed one piece of candy when you thought you ordered an entire bag.

To Convert		Do the Math		
liters (l) to gallons,	multiply by 0.26	4 liters x 0.26	=	1.04 gallons
gallons to liters,	multiply by 3.79	10 gal. x 3.79	=	37.9 liters
kilograms (kg) to pounds,	multiply by 2.2	2 kilograms x 2.2	=	4.4 pounds
pounds to kilos,	multiply by 0.46	10 pounds x 0.46	=	4.6 kg
grams (g) to ounces,	multiply by 0.035	100 grams x 0.035	=	3.5 oz.
ounces to grams,	multiply by 28.35	10 oz. x 28.35	=	283.5 g.
meters (m) to feet,	multiply by 3.28	2 meters x 3.28	=	6.56 feet
feet to meters,	multiply by 0.3	6 feet x 0.3	=	1.8 meters

For fun, take your weight in pounds and convert it into kilograms. It sounds better that way, doesn't it? How many kilometers is it from your home to school, to work, to the post office?

The Simple Versions		
one liter	=	approximately one US quart
four liters	=	approximately one US gallon
one kilo	=	approximately 2.2 pounds
100 grams	=	approximately 3.5 ounces
500 grams	=	slightly more than one pound
one meter	=	slightly more than three feet

The distance between **New York e Roma è** approximately 4,278 miles. How many kilometers would that be? It is only 907 miles between **London e Roma**. How many kilometers is that?

kilometers (km.) to miles,	multiply by 0.62	1000 km. x 0.62	=	620 miles
miles to kilometers,	multiply by 1.6	1000 miles x 1.6	=	1,600 km.

Inches	1	2	3	4	5	6	7

To convert centimeters into inches, multiply by 0.39   Example: 9 cm. x 0.39 = 3.51 in.

To convert inches into centimeters, multiply by 2.54   Example: 4 in. x 2.54 = 10.16 cm.

cm 1	2	3	4	5	6	7	8	9	10	11	12	13	14	15	16	17	18

(kohn-toh)
Il Conto
bill

Sì, ci sono anche bills to pay **in Italia. Lei** have just finished your delicious dinner **e Lei**
(chee)
there are   also

(vor-reb-beh) *(fah)*   *(kah-meh-ree-eh-reh)*   *(kah-meh-ree-eh-rah)*   *(kah-meh-ree-eh-reh)*
vorrebbe pagare. Che fa? Lei call for **il cameriere** **o la cameriera.** **Il cameriere**
would like   do you do   waiter   waitress   waiter

will normally reel off what **Lei ha** eaten while writing rapidly. **Lui** will then place a piece **di**
he

carta sulla tavola, "Fa venti euro." Lei will pay **il cameriere o** perhaps **Lei** will pay **alla cassa.**
it makes (comes to)   cashier's desk

Being a seasoned traveler, **Lei** know that tipping **in Italia** is the same as tipping in America. If

(sair-vee-tsee-oh)
il servizio is not included on **il conto,** leave what you consider an appropriate amount for your
service

(soo-oh) (vee-ah-joh)
cameriere sulla tavola. When **Lei** dine out on **Suo viaggio,** it is always a good idea to make
your   trip

a reservation. It can be difficult to get into a popular **ristorante.** Nevertheless, the experience

is well worth the trouble **Lei** might encounter to obtain a reservation. **E** remember, **Lei** know

enough **italiano** to make a reservation. Just speak slowly and clearly.

❑ **sincero** *(seen-cheh-roh)*	sincere		_____
❑ **la sinfonia** *(seen-foh-nee-ah)*	symphony		_____
❑ **il soggetto** *(soh-jet-toh)*	subject	**S**	_____
❑ **solo** *(soh-loh)*	alone, solitary		_____
❑ **la somma** *(sohm-mah)*	total, sum		_____

Remember these key **parole** when dining out **all'italiana.** *(ahl-lee-tahl-yah-nah)*
in the Italian manner

(kah-meh-ree-eh-reh)
il cameriere _____
waiter

(kah-meh-ree-eh-rah)
la cameriera _____
waitress

(kohn-toh)
il conto *il conto, il conto, il conto*
bill

(mahn-chah)
la mancia _____
tip

(meh-noo) *(lee-stah)*
il menù/ la lista _____
menu

(preh-goh)
prego _____
you're welcome

(mee)(skoo-zee)
mi scusi _____
excuse me

(grah-tsee-eh)
grazie _____
thank you

(pair)(fah-voh-reh) *(pee-ah-cheh-reh)*
per favore / per piacere _____
please

(mee)(dee-ah)
mi dia _____
give me

Ecco una sample **conversazione** involving paying **il conto.**

Gianni:	**Mi scusi. Vorrei pagare il conto, per favore.** to pay _____ *Mi scusi. Vorrei pagare il conto, per favore.* _____
(lahl-bair-gah-toh-reh) **L'albergatore:** hotelkeeper	**Che camera, per favore?** *(keh)* what room _____
Gianni:	**Numero trecentodieci.** _____
L'albergatore:	**Grazie. Un momento, per piacere.** _____
L'albergatore:	**Ecco il conto.** _____

If **Lei ha** any **problema con i numeri** just ask someone to write out **la somma** so that **Lei** can *(sohm-mah)*
sum

be sure you understand everything correctly, **"Per favore, mi scriva la somma."** *(mee) (skree-vah)*
for me write

Practice: _____
(Please write the sum for me.)

❏ **la sorpresa** *(sor-preh-zah)* . . . . surprise
❏ **lo spagnolo** *(spahn-yoh-loh)* . . . . Spanish, Spaniard
❏ **lo spettacolo** *(spet-tah-koh-loh)* . . . . spectacle, show **S**
❏ **gli Stati Uniti** *(stah-tee)(oo-nee-tee)* . . . . United States
❏ **lo straniero** *(strah-nee-eh-roh)* . . . . foreigner

_____
_____
_____
_____
_____

Adesso, let's take a break from **i conti e il denaro** e learn some **nuove** fun **parole.** **Lei** can
money   new

always practice these **parole** by using your flash cards at the back of this **libro.** Carry these

flash cards in your purse, pocket, briefcase **o** knapsack **e** *use them!*

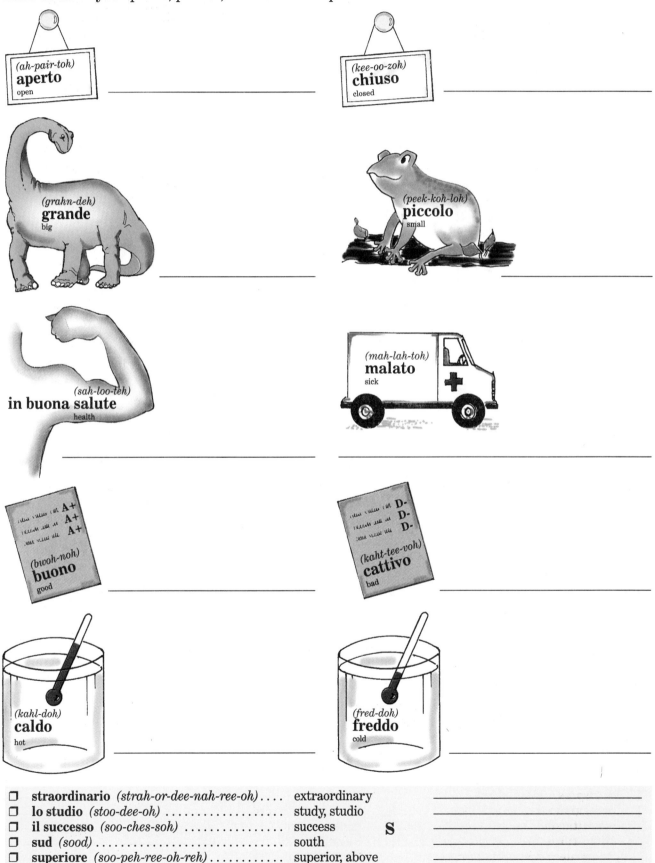

(ah-pair-toh)
aperto
open

_____

(kee-oo-zoh)
chiuso
closed

_____

(grahn-deh)
grande
big

_____

(peek-koh-loh)
piccolo
small

_____

(sah-loo-teh)
in buona salute
health

_____

(mah-lah-toh)
malato
sick

_____

(bwoh-noh)
buono
good

_____

(kaht-tee-voh)
cattivo
bad

_____

(kahl-doh)
caldo
hot

_____

(fred-doh)
freddo
cold

_____

❏ **straordinario** *(strah-or-dee-nah-ree-oh)*	extraordinary	_____
❏ **lo studio** *(stoo-dee-oh)*	study, studio	_____
❏ **il successo** *(soo-ches-soh)*	success	**S** _____
❏ **sud** *(sood)*	south	_____
❏ **superiore** *(soo-peh-ree-oh-reh)*	superior, above	_____

71

(kor-toh)
corto _____
short

(loon-goh)
lungo _____
long

(len-toh)
lento _____
slow

(veh-loh-cheh) (rah-pee-doh)
veloce / rapido _____
fast

(ahl-toh)
alto _____
tall

(bahs-soh)
basso _____
short

(vek-kee-oh)
vecchio _____
old

(joh-vah-neh)
giovane _____
young

(kah-roh)
caro _____
expensive

(eh-koh-noh-mee-koh)
economico _____
inexpensive

(reek-koh)
ricco _____
rich

(poh-veh-roh)
povero _____
poor

(mohl-toh)
molto _____
a lot

(poh-koh)
poco _____
a little

- ❏ **il tabacco** *(tah-bahk-koh)* .... tobacco
- ❏ **il tassì** *(tahs-see)* .... taxi
- ❏ **il tavolo** *(tah-voh-loh)* .... table
- — **la tavola calda** .... cafeteria
- ❏ **il teatro** *(teh-ah-troh)* .... theater

t _____
_____
_____
_____

Ecco **dei** *(deh-ee)* **verbi nuovi.**
some

(sah-peh-reh)
sapere _____
to know (fact)

(leh-jeh-reh)
leggere _____
to read

(poh-teh-reh)
potere _____
to be able to, can

(doh-veh-reh)
dovere _____
to have to, must, to owe

Study the patterns below closely, as **Lei** will use these verbs a lot.

Via Cavour

(sah-peh-reh)
sapere
to know

Io *so/* _____ **tutto.**
everything

(leen-dee-ree-tsoh)
Lei *sa/* _____ **l'indirizzo.**
address

Lui *sa/* _____ **parlare l'italiano.**
Lei (she)   to speak

Noi *sappiamo/* _____ **ordinare una birra.**

Loro *sanno/* _____ **parlare l'inglese.**

Come va?

(poh-teh-reh)
potere
to be able to, can

Io *posso/* _____ **comprare un biglietto.**

(kah-pee-reh)
Lei *può/* _____ **capire l'inglese.**
understand

(moo-zeh-oh)
Lui *può/* _____ **vedere il museo.**
Lei (she)

(jeh-oh-meh-tree-ah)
Noi *possiamo/* **imparare la geometria.**

(mah-reh)
Loro *possono/* _____ **vedere il mare.**
sea

(leh-jeh-reh)
leggere
to read

Io _____ **il libro.**

(jor-nah-leh)
Lei _____ **il giornale.**
newspaper

Lui _____ **la lista.**
Lei (she)   menu

Noi *leggiamo/* _____ **molto.**
a lot

Loro _____ **la rivista.**
magazine

(doh-veh-reh)
dovere
to have to, must, to owe

(kohn-toh)
Io *devo/* _____ **pagare il conto.**
bill

Lei *deve/* _____ **vedere il Colosseo.**

Lui *deve/* _____ **scrivere due lettere.**
Lei (she)

(lahl-bair-goh)
Noi *dobbiamo/* _____ **trovare l'albergo.**

(vee-zee-tah-reh)
Loro *devono/* _____ **visitare Roma.**
visit

❑ **il telefono** *(teh-leh-foh-noh)*	telephone	_____
❑ **il telegramma** *(teh-leh-grahm-mah)*	telegram	_____
❑ **il televisore** *(teh-leh-vee-zoh-reh)*	television set **t**	_____
❑ **la temperatura** *(tem-peh-rah-too-rah)*	temperature	_____
❑ **il Tevere** *(teh-veh-reh)*	Tiber River	_____

Notice that "**sapere**," "**dovere**," "**potere**," **e** "**vorrei**" can be combined with another verb.

Vorrei visitare Pisa.
(I) would like

Vorremmo bere due birre.
          drink

Posso comprare un libro.
(I) can

Possiamo comprare una casa.

Devo visitare Roma.
(I) must

Dobbiamo pagare il conto.

              (eem-pah-rah-reh)
Vorrei imparare l'italiano.
(I) would like

Posso visitare Roma.
(I) can

Devo imparare l'italiano.
(I) must

So parlare l'italiano.
(I) know how to

(pwoh)   *(kwee)*
Può you translate the sentences **qui sotto in italiano? Le risposte sono qui sotto.**
can   here

1. I know how to speak Italian. _____

2. They must pay the bill. _____

3. He has to pay the bill. _____

4. We know the address. _____ Sappiamo l'indirizzo. _____

5. She knows a lot. _____

6. We know how to read Italian. _____

7. I cannot find the hotel. _____

8. We do not understand French. _____

9. I would like to visit Rome. _____

10. She reads the newspaper. _____

74

Adesso, draw **linee** *(lee-neh-eh)* **fra** the opposites **qui sotto.** **Non** forget to say them out loud. Use these
lines between

parole every day to describe **le cose nella Sua casa, nella Sua scuola** *(skoo-oh-lah)* **e nel Suo ufficio.**
your home school

(grahn-deh)
grande

(see-nee-strah)
sinistra

(joh-vah-neh)
giovane

(poh-veh-roh)
povero

(sah-loo-teh)
in buona salute

(loon-goh)
lungo

(mohl-toh)
molto

(bwoh-noh)
buono

(kee-oo-zoh)
chiuso

(soht-toh)
sotto

(kahl-doh)
caldo

(kah-roh)
caro

(len-toh)
lento

(soh-prah)
sopra

(kaht-tee-voh)
cattivo

(peek-koh-loh)
piccolo

(eh-koh-noh-mee-koh)
economico

(kor-toh)
corto

(mah-lah-toh)
malato

(ah-pair-toh)
aperto

(vek-kee-oh)
vecchio

(veh-loh-cheh)
veloce

(deh-strah)
destra

(poh-koh)
poco

(reek-koh)
ricco

(fred-doh)
freddo

❑ **la terrazza** *(tair-rah-tsah)*	terrace	_____
❑ **il tesoro** *(teh-zoh-roh)*	treasure	_____
❑ **il titolo** *(tee-toh-loh)*	title	**t** _____
❑ **la torre** *(tor-reh)*	tower	_____
— **La Torre Pendente**	Leaning Tower (of Pisa)	_____

19

Il Viaggiatore Viaggia
(vee-ah-jah-toh-reh) *(vee-ah-jah)*
traveler   travels

(ee-eh-ree)
Ieri a Venezia!
yesterday

(oh-jee)
Oggi a Firenze!
today

(doh-mah-nee)
Domani a Milano!
tomorrow

If you know a few key **parole,** traveling can be easy and quite efficient **in Italia. L'Italia non è**

grande, therefore **il viaggio è molto facile** within the distinctive "boot" **che si chiama**
(fah-chee-leh)   *(keh) (see) (kee-ah-mah)*
easy   that is called

"l'Italia." Come viaggiare in Italia?
(vee-ah-jah-reh)
to travel

Stefano viaggia in macchina.
(vee-ah-jah) *(mahk-kee-nah)*
travels   car

Franca viaggia in treno.

Francesca viaggia in aereo.
(ah-eh-reh-oh)
airplane

Anna viaggia in nave.
(nah-veh)
boat

Andrea viaggia in motocicletta.
(moh-toh-chee-klet-tah)

Silvia viaggia in autobus.

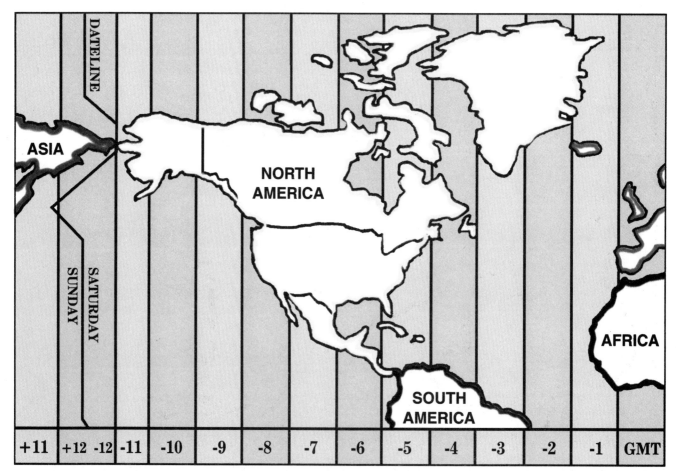

+11	+12	-12	-11	-10	-9	-8	-7	-6	-5	-4	-3	-2	-1	GMT

ASIA   NORTH AMERICA   AFRICA   SOUTH AMERICA   DATELINE   SATURDAY SUNDAY

Quando Lei are traveling, **Lei** will want to tell others your nationality **e Lei** will meet people from all corners of the world. Can you guess where people are from if they say one of the following? **Le risposte** are in your glossary beginning on page 108.

(dahl-leen-gheel-tair-rah)
Io vengo dall'Inghilterra. _____
come   from

(ven-ee-ah-moh)   *(frahn-chah)*
Noi veniamo dalla Francia. _____
we   come

(ven-goh)   *(toor-kee-ah)*
Vengo dalla Turchia. _____
(I) come

(jair-mahn-yah)
Veniamo dalla Germania. _____
(we) come

(greh-chah)
Vengo dalla Grecia. _____

(dahl-leer-lahn-dah)
Veniamo dall'Irlanda. _____

(dahl-lah-oo-stree-ah)
Vengo dall'Austria. _____

(dahl-leez-rah-eh-leh)
Lei viene dall'Israele. _____
she   comes

(zveet-tsair-ah)
Vengo dalla Svizzera. _____

(jahp-poh-neh)
Lui viene dal Giappone. _____
he

(dahl-lah-oo-strahl-yah)
Vengo dall'Australia. _____

(roos-see-ah)
Lui viene dalla Russia. _____

(dahl-yee) (stah-tee) (oo-nee-tee)
Vengo dagli Stati Uniti. _____

Lui viene dalla Spagna. _____
he   comes

(sood-ah-free-kah)
Vengo dal Sudafrica. _____

(kah-nah-dah)
Vengo dal Canada. _____

-1	GMT	+1	+2	+3	+4	+5	+6	+7	+8	+9	+10	+11	+12 -12

Gli Italiani enjoy going on **vacanze,** *(vah-kahn-tseh)* vacation   so it is no **sorpresa** *(sor-preh-zah)* surprise   to find **molte parole** built on **la parola "viaggiare,"** *(vee-ah-jah-reh)* which means "to travel." Practice saying **le parole seguenti** *(seh-gwen-tee)* following   many times. **Lei** will use them **spesso.** *(spes-soh)* often

(vee-ah-jah-reh)
viaggiare _____
to travel

(ah-jen-tsee-ah) *(vee-ah-jee)*
un'agenzia   di viaggi _____
travel agency

(vee-ah-jah-toh-reh)
il viaggiatore _____
traveler

(bwohn) (vee-ah-joh)
Buon Viaggio! _____
have a good trip

If **Lei viaggia in macchina,** here are a few key **parole.**

(lah-oo-toh-strah-dah)
l'autostrada _____
freeway

(mahk-kee-nah) (noh-leh-jah-reh)
una macchina da noleggiare _____
rental car

(strah-dah)
la strada _____
street, road

(ah-jen-tsee-ah) (noh-leh-joh)
un'agenzia   di noleggio _____
car rental agency

(par-kee-meh-troh)
il parchimetro _____
parking meter

(dee-skoh) (soh-stah)
il disco di sosta _____
parking disk

Sotto ci *(chee)* **sono** some basic signs which **Lei** should also learn to recognize quickly.

(en-trah-reh)
entrare _____
to enter

(oo-shee-reh)
uscire _____
to exit

L'ENTRATA ➡

L'USCITA ➡

(len-trah-tah) (leen-gres-soh)
l'entrata or **l'ingresso** _____
entrance

(loo-shee-tah)
l'uscita _____
exit

(preen-chee-pah-leh)
l'entrata principale _____
main

(see-koo-reh-tsah)
l'uscita di sicurezza _____
emergency exit

SPINGERE

TIRARE

(speen-jeh-reh)
spingere _____
push (doors)

(tee-rah-reh)
tirare _____
pull (doors)

❑ **il tram** *(trahm)*	tram, street car	_____
❑ **tranquillo** *(trahn-kweel-loh)*	calm, tranquil	_____
❑ **tre** *(treh)*	three	**t** _____
❑ **il treno** *(treh-noh)*	train	_____
❑ **il turista** *(too-ree-stah)*	tourist	_____

Let's learn the basic travel verbs. Take out a piece of paper **e** make up your own sentences

with these **parole nuove.** Follow the same pattern as in previous Steps.

(ahn-dah-reh) *(ah-eh-reh-oh)*
andare **in aereo** _____
to fly

(gwee-dah-reh) *(mahk-kee-nah)*
guidare/andare in macchina _____
to drive

(ar-ree-vah-reh)
arrivare _____
to arrive

(par-tee-reh)
partire _____
to depart, to leave

(preh-noh-tah-reh)
prenotare _____
to reserve, to book

(fah-reh) *(vah-lee-jeh)*
fare **le valigie** _____
to pack   suitcases

(cheh) *(chee) (soh-noh)*
c'è / ci sono _____
there is   there are

(kahm-bee-ah-reh)
cambiare _____
to transfer (vehicles) or to change money!

Ecco some **parole nuove per il Suo** *(soo-oh)* **viaggio.**
                                         trip

(lah-eh-reh-oh-por-toh)
l'aereoporto
airport

(mar-chah-pee-eh-deh) *(bee-nah-ree-oh)*
il marciapiede or **il binario**
platform   train track

(loh-rah-ree-oh)
l'orario
timetable

Milano - Roma		
Partenza	Treno	Arrivo
00:41	50	09:41
07:40	19	15:40
12:15	22	00:15
14:32	10	23:32
21:40	04	09:40

(stah-tsee-oh-neh) (deh-ee)
la stazione dei treni
train station

❏ **l'ufficio** *(loof-fee-choh)* . . . . office _____
❏ **ultimo** *(ool-tee-moh)* . . . . last, final, ultimate _____
❏ **unico** *(oo-nee-koh)* . . . . unique, only _____ **u**
— **senso unico** . . . . one-way (traffic) _____
❏ **universale** *(oo-nee-vair-sah-leh)* . . . . universal _____

Con these **parole, Lei è** ready for any **viaggio**, anywhere. **Lei** should have no problem **con**

(vee-ah-joh)
are

these new verbs, just remember the basic "plug-in" formula **Lei** have already learned. Use

that knowledge to translate the following thoughts **in italiano. Le risposte sono qui sotto.**

into

1. I fly (go by plane) to Rome. _____
2. I transfer trains in Milan. _____
3. He drives to Padua. _____
4. We arrive tomorrow. _____
5. We buy tickets to Pisa. _____
6. They drive to Florence. _____
7. Where is the train to Trieste? _____
8. How can you fly (go by plane) to Italy? With American or with Alitalia? _____

_____

Ecco some **parole importanti per il viaggiatore.**

(vee-ah-jah-toh-reh)
traveler

Bologna - Firenze		
Partenza	**Treno**	**Arrivo**
02:41	103	08:30
09:40	233	14:15
14:15	33	19:00
16:32	43	09:40
23:30	53	05:55

(ohk-koo-pah-toh)
occupato _____
occupied

(lee-beh-roh)
libero _____
free

(skohm-par-tee-men-toh)
lo scompartimento _____
compartment, wagon

(poh-stoh)
il posto _____
seat

(par-ten-tsah)
la partenza _____
departure

(lar-ree-voh)
l' arrivo _____
arrival

(een-tair-nah-tsee-oh-nah-leh)
internazionale _____
international

(nah-tsee-oh-nah-leh)
nazionale _____
domestic

Increase your travel **parole** by writing out **le parole** *(kwee)* **qui** sotto e practicing the sample sentences out loud. Practice asking **domande con "dove."** It will help you later.

(pair)
per_____
to, for

Dov'è il treno per Roma?

(beel-yet-toh)
il biglietto_____
ticket

Quanto costa un biglietto?

(loof-fee-choh) (oh-jet-tee) (zmar-ree-tee)
l'ufficio oggetti smarriti_____
lost-and-found office

Dov'è l'ufficio oggetti smarriti?

(fahk-kee-noh)
il facchino_____
porter

Dov'è il facchino?

(voh-loh)
il volo_____ *Dov'è il volo per Catania?* _____
flight

Dov'è il volo per Catania?

(deh-poh-zee-toh) (bah-gahl-yee)
il deposito bagagli_____
left-luggage office

Dov'è un deposito bagagli?

(loof-fee-choh) (kahm-bee-oh)
l'ufficio di cambio_____
money-exchange office

Dov'è l'ufficio di cambio?

(spor-tel-loh)
lo sportello_____
counter, ticket window

Dov'è lo sportello numero otto?

(dah-spet-toh)
la sala d'aspetto_____
waiting room

Dov'è la sala d'aspetto?

(vah-goh-neh) (ree-stoh-rahn-teh)
il vagone ristorante_____
dining car

Dov'è il vagone ristorante?

(let-toh)
il vagone letto_____
sleeping car

Dov'è il vagone letto numero due?

(foo-mah-reh)
fumare_____
to smoke

È vietato fumare?
prohibited

_____ **arriva il treno?**   _____ **è?**
(when)   (when)   (what)   (what)   is it

☐ **l'università** *(loo-nee-vair-see-tah)*	university	
☐ **urbano** *(oor-bah-noh)*	urban	**u** _____
☐ **usato** *(oo-zah-toh)*	used, second-hand	_____
☐ **usuale** *(oo-zoo-ah-leh)*	usual, customary	_____
☐ **l'utensile** *(loo-ten-see-leh)*	utensil	_____

81

(pwoh)
Può leggere le frasi seguenti?
can you read   sentences following

⟵ **Lei è adesso seduto nell'aereoplano**
          (seh-doo-toh)
          seated

e Lei viaggia in Italia. Lei ha il denaro,

il Suo biglietto, il Suo passaporto e le Sue

valigie. Adesso, è un turista. Lei arriva
suitcases   tourist

domani alle sei. Buon viaggio! Buon

divertimento!

In Italia there are many different types of trains — **il treno locale è lento; il diretto è**
                                                              (loh-kah-leh)   *(dee-ret-toh)*
                                                              local   direct

rapido e both **il rapido e l'espresso** are **molto rapidi.** If **Lei** plan to travel a long distance, **Lei**

may wish to catch an Inter-City **treno o** a TEE or TEN train which travels faster **e** makes

fewer intermediate stops.

❒ **le vacanze** *(vah-kahn-tseh)*	vacation	_____
— **fare le vacanze**	to go on vacation	_____
❒ **la vaccinazione** *(vah-chee-nah-tsee-oh-neh)* .	vaccination **V**	_____
❒ **la vaniglia** *(vah-neel-yah)*	vanilla	_____
❒ **il vaporetto** *(vah-poh-ret-toh)*	steam ferry (in Venice)	_____

Knowing these travel **parole** will make your holiday twice as enjoyable **e** at least three times as easy. Review these **parole** by doing the crossword puzzle **qui sotto.** Drill yourself on this Step by selecting other destinations **e** ask your own **domande** about **i treni, gli autobus o gli aereoplani** that go there. Select **le parole nuove dal Suo dizionario e** ask your own questions beginning with **quando, dove, e quanto costa. Le risposte** to the crossword puzzle are at the bottom of the next page.

ACROSS
1. to rent (as in a car)
2. have a good trip
3. to smoke
4. occupied
5. timetable
6. money
7. foreigner
8. flight
9. nothing
10. time
11. street, road
12. to leave
13. arrival
14. entrance
15. station
16. to reserve
17. to go
18. domestic

DOWN
1. we/us
2. to drive
3. money-exchange
4. prohibited
5. track
6. exit
7. train
8. you (plural!)
9. ticket window
10. free
11. traveler
12. passport
13. departure

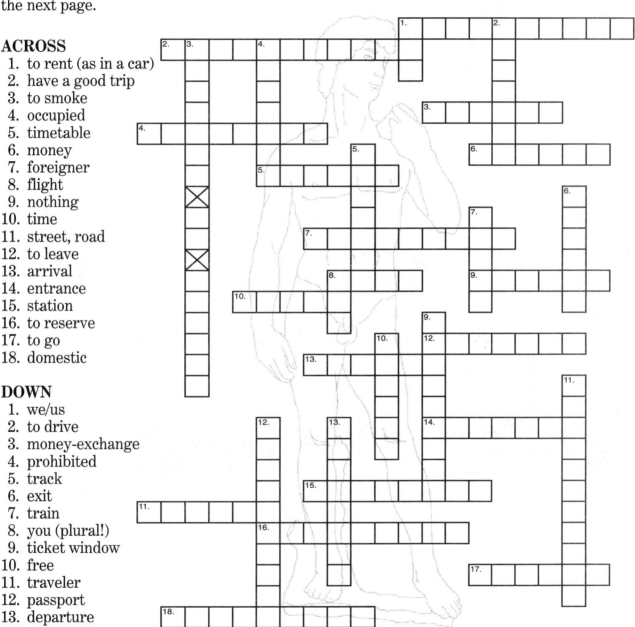

Davide – Michelangelo's famous figure dating from the 16th century. **Davide** is part of the collection of the Academy Gallery in Florence.

❏ **la varietà** *(vah-ree-eh-tah)* . . . . variety   _____
❏ **il vaso** *(vah-zoh)* . . . . vase   _____
❏ **la vena** *(veh-nah)* . . . . vein   **V** _____
❏ **il venditore** *(ven-dee-toh-reh)* . . . . vendor, seller   _____
❏ **la versione** *(vair-zee-oh-neh)* . . . . version   _____

What about inquiring about il **prezzo** dei **biglietti?** **Lei può** ask these **domande.**

(preh-tsoh) price   _(beel-yet-tee)_ tickets   _(pwoh)_ can

(kwahn-toh)
Quanto è il biglietto per Taranto?_____

Quanto è il biglietto per Napoli?_____

Quanto è il biglietto per Ravenna? _____

(sem-plee-cheh)
semplice _____
one-way

(ahn-dah-tah)   _(ree-tor-noh)_
andata e ritorno_____
round trip

What about times of **partenze e arrivi?** **Lei può** ask this as well.

(par-ten-tseh) departure   _(ar-ree-vee)_ arrival

(keh)   _(par-teh)_
A che ora parte il treno per Bari?_____
when   departs   for

(ar-ree-vah)   _(pah-ree-jee)_
A che ora arriva il treno da Parigi? _____

A che ora arriva l'aereoplano da New York? _____
arrives   from

A che ora parte l'aereoplano per Roma?_____

A che ora parte il treno per Rimini? _____

Lei have just arrived in Italia. **Lei è alla stazione. Dove vorrebbe andare? A Lecce?**
(vor-reb-beh) would you like   to go

A Orvieto? Tell that to the person at **lo sportello** selling **i biglietti!**
window

(see-eh-nah)
Vorrei andare a Siena. _____
to go

A che ora parte il treno per Siena?_____

Quanto costa il biglietto per Siena? _____

LE RISPOSTE

ACROSS
1. noleggiare
2. buon viaggio
3. fumare
4. occupato
5. orario
6. denaro
7. straniero
8. volo
9. niente
10. tempo
11. strada
12. partire
13. arrivo
14. entrata
15. stazione
16. prenotare
17. andare
18. nazionale

DOWN
1. noi
2. guidare
3. ufficio di cambio
4. vietato
5. binario
6. uscita
7. treno
8. voi
9. sportello
10. libero
11. viaggiatore
12. passaporto
13. partenza

84

Adesso that **Lei** know the essential words for traveling **in Italia** – what are some speciality items **Lei** might go in search of?

(pel-let-tair-ee-ah)
la pelletteria
leather goods

(joy-el-lee)
i gioielli
jewelry

(cheh-rah-mee-keh)
le ceramiche
pottery

(skar-peh)
le scarpe
shoes

(veh-stee-tee)
i vestiti
clothing

(proh-foo-mee)
i profumi
perfume

Consider using ITALIAN *a language map*™ as well. ITALIAN *a language map*™ is the perfect companion for your travels when **Lei** may not wish to take along this **libro**. Each section focuses on essentials for your **viaggio.** Your *Language Map*™ is not meant to replace learning **italiano**, but will help you in the event **Lei** forget something and need a little bit of help. For more information about the *Language Map*™ Series, please turn to page 132.

❏ **la vergine** *(vair-jee-neh)* . . . . virgin
— **la Santa Vergine** . . . . Holy Virgin
❏ **la via** *(vee-ah); via* . . . . way; by
— **via Appia Antica** . . . . Appian Way
— **via aerea** . . . . by air, airmail

V

20

(meh-noo) *(lee-stah)*
Il Menù o La Lista
menu

Adesso Lei è in Italia e Lei ha una camera. Lei ha fame. *(fah-meh)* **Dov'è un buon ristorante?** First
hunger

of all, **ci sono** different types of places to eat. Let's learn them.
there are

(ree-stoh-rahn-teh)
il ristorante _____

exactly what it says with a variety of meals and prices

(traht-toh-ree-ah)
la trattoria _____

usually less elegant and less expensive than a **ristorante,** often run by a family

(loh-steh-ree-ah)
l'osteria _____

found in the country or in small towns, serves mostly drinks and easy-to-prepare food

(tah-voh-lah) (kahl-dah)
la tavola calda _____

similar to a cafeteria, with a variety of foods

il bar _____

serves pastries and sandwiches, concentrates on liquid refreshments
(great place for morning coffee or tea)

If **Lei** look around you **nel ristorante italiano, Lei** will see that some **costumi italiani** might
(koh-stoo-mee)
customs

be different from yours. Sharing **tavole con** others **è** a common **e molto** pleasant custom.

Before beginning your **pasto,** be sure to wish those sharing your table – "**Buon appetito!**"
(pah-stoh) *(bwohn) (ahp-peh-tee-toh)*
meal   enjoy your meal

Your turn to practice now.

_____
(enjoy your meal)

And at least one more time for practice!

_____
(enjoy your meal)

❏ **vigoroso** *(vee-goh-roh-zoh)* .... vigorous _____
❏ **il vino** *(vee-noh)* .... wine _____
❏ **la visita** *(vee-zee-tah)* .... visit   **v** _____
  — fare una visita .... to pay a visit _____
❏ **la vitamina** *(vee-tah-mee-nah)* .... vitamin _____

Start imagining now all the new taste treats you will experience abroad. Try all of the different

types of eating establishments. Experiment. If **Lei trova un ristorante** that **Lei** would like to

try, consider calling ahead to make a **prenotazione.** *(preh-noh-tah-tsee-oh-neh)* **"Vorrei fare una prenotazione."** If **Lei**

ha bisogno di una lista, catch the attention of **il cameriere,** *(kah-meh-ree-eh-reh)* ^{to make} by saying,

"Cameriere! La lista, per favore."

_____
(Waiter! The menu, please.)

If your **cameriere** asks if **Lei** enjoyed your

pasto, a smile **e** a **"Sì, grazie"** will tell him

that you did.

Most **ristoranti italiani** post **la lista** outside **o** inside. Do not hesitate to ask to see **la lista**

before being seated so **Lei sa** what type of **pasti e prezzi Lei** will encounter. Most **ristoranti**

_{know}   _{meals} _{prices}

offer **una lista a prezzo** *(preh-tsoh)* **fisso.** This is a complete **pasto** at a fair **prezzo.** Always look for the

_{fixed}   _{price}

(pee-aht-toh) *(jor-noh)*
piatto del giorno as well.
_{daily special}

❐ **zero** *(zeh-roh)*	zero	_____
❐ **lo zodiaco** *(zoh-dee-ah-koh)*	zodiac	_____
— Sono del segno acquario	I'm an Aquarius. **Z**	_____
❐ **la zona** *(zoh-nah)*	zone	_____
❐ **lo zoo** *(dzoh)*	zoo	_____

In Italia, ci sono tre main **pasti** *(pah-stee)* meals to enjoy every day, plus perhaps **un dolce** *(dohl-cheh)* pastry **per** for the tired
(vee-ah-jah-toh-reh) **viaggiatore** **nel** *(poh-meh-ree-joh)* **pomeriggio.** afternoon

la colazione *(koh-lah-tsee-oh-neh)* **/ la prima colazione** _____
breakfast

This meal usually consists of **caffè o tè e pane** or a sweet roll, butter and marmalade.

Check serving times before **Lei** retire for the night or you might miss out!

il pranzo *(prahn-tsoh)* _____
mid-day meal

generally served from 12:00 to 14:00; this is the big meal of the day.

la cena *(cheh-nah)* _____
evening meal

generally served from 19:30 to 22:00; this is a light meal.

Adesso for a preview of delights to come . . . At the back of this **libro, Lei** will find a sample

lista italiana. Legga la lista oggi e impari le parole nuove! When **Lei** are ready to leave
read   today   learn

on your **viaggio,** cut out **la lista,** fold it, **e** carry it in your pocket, wallet **o** purse. Before you go,

how do **Lei** say these **tre** phrases which are so very important for the hungry traveler?

Excuse me. I would like to make a reservation. _____

Waiter! The menu, please. _____

Enjoy your meal! _____

_____ **mangia l'insalata?** *(mahn-jah)*   _____ **beve tè?**
(who)   eats   (who)   drinks

_____ **viaggia a Venezia?**
(who)

___ (who)

Learning the following should help you to identify what kind of meat **Lei** have ordered **e come** it will be prepared.

☐ **il manzo** *(mahn-tsoh)* . . . . beef _____
☐ **il vitello** *(vee-tel-loh)* . . . . veal _____
☐ **il maiale** *(my-ah-leh)* . . . . pork _____
☐ **l'agnello** *(lahn-yel-loh)* . . . . lamb _____

Il menù below has the main categories **Lei** will find in most restaurants. Learn them **oggi** so that **Lei** will easily recognize them when you dine **a Roma, Siena o Ravenna.** Be sure to write the words in the blanks below.

(meh-noo)
Menù

(ahn-tee-pah-stee)
antipasti
appetizers

_____

(zoop-peh)
zuppe
soups

_____

(oo-oh-vah)
uova
eggs

_____

(peh-sheh)
pesce
fish

_____

(pee-aht-tee) *(jor-noh)*
piatti del giorno
daily specials

_____

(pah-stah-shoot-tah)
pastasciutta
pasta

_____

(ree-zoh)
riso
rice

_____

(een-sah-lah-teh)
insalate
salads

_____

(dohl-chee)
dolci
desserts

_____

(vair-doo-rah)
verdura
vegetables

_____

(froot-tah)
frutta
fruit

_____

(for-mah-joh)
formaggio
cheese

_____

(beh-vahn-deh)
bevande
beverages

_____

❑	**il pollame** *(pohl-lah-meh)*	poultry	_____
❑	**il montone** *(mohn-toh-neh)*	mutton	_____
❑	**la cacciagione** *(kah-chah-joh-neh)*	game	_____
❑	**fritto** *(freet-toh)*	fried	_____
❑	**arrosto** *(ar-roh-stoh)*	roasted	_____

Lei may also order **verdura** *(vair-doo-rah)* **con il Suo pasto** or perhaps **un'insalata verde.** *(vair-deh)* One day at an open-air **mercato** *(mair-kah-toh)* will teach you **i nomi** for all the different kinds of **verdura e frutta,** *(froot-tah)* plus it will be a delightful experience for you. **Lei può** always consult your menu guide at the back of **questo libro** if **Lei** forget **il nome corretto. Adesso Lei** are seated **e il cameriere** arrives.

vegetables ... *meal* ... *green* ... *fruit* ... *can* ... *this* ... *waiter*

> **La lista, per favore.**

> **E come bevanda?**

> **Un bicchiere di vino bianco, per piacere.**

La prima colazione è un po' differente *(poh)* because it is fairly standardized **e Lei** will frequently take it **nel Suo albergo** as **è generalmente** included **nel prezzo della Sua camera. Qui sotto c'è** a sample of what **Lei può** expect to greet you **la mattina.** *(maht-tee-nah)*

breakfast ... a ... little ... in the morning

Bevande

caffè

tè

caffellatte
coffee and steamed milk

cioccolata

succo di arancia
juice · orange

succo di pomodoro
tomato

succo di pompelmo
grapefruit

latte

e . . .

pane

panino
roll

burro

marmellata
jam

prosciutto
ham

salsiccia
sausage

frittata
omelette

formaggio
cheese

- ❑ **cotto** *(koht-toh)* . . . . cooked
- ❑ **al forno** *(ahl)(for-noh)* . . . . baked
- ❑ **alla griglia** *(ahl-lah)(greel-yah)* . . . . grilled
- ❑ **farcito** *(far-chee-toh)* . . . . stuffed
- ❑ **bollito** *(bohl-lee-toh)* . . . . boiled

Ecco an example of what **Lei** might select for your evening meal. Using your menu guide on pages 117 and 118, as well as what **Lei** have learned in this Step, fill in the blanks *in English* with what **Lei** believe your **cameriere** will bring you. **Le risposte sono sotto.**

Antipasti
Antipasto misto

_____

Insalate
Insalata verde

_____

Piatto del Giorno
Vitello al pomodoro

_____

Dolci
Frutta di stagione

_____

(when) (how) (why)

LE RISPOSTE

Appetizers:	Assorted Appetizers
Salads:	Green salad
Entrées:	Veal in an Herbal Tomato Sauce
Desserts:	Seasonal Fruit

Adesso is a good time for a quick review. Draw lines between **le parole italiane e** their English equivalents.

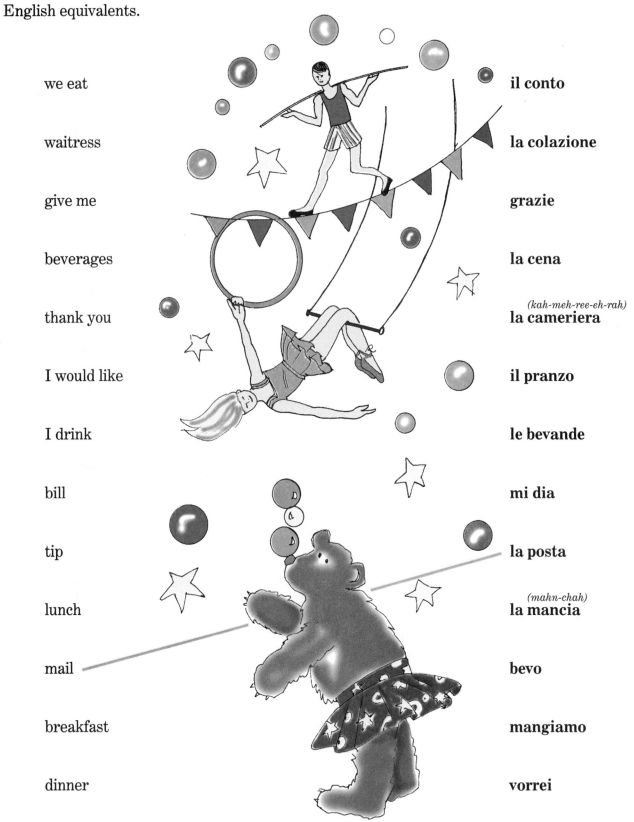

we eat	**il conto**
waitress	**la colazione**
give me	**grazie**
beverages	**la cena**
thank you	*(kah-meh-ree-eh-rah)* **la cameriera**
I would like	**il pranzo**
I drink	**le bevande**
bill	**mi dia**
tip	**la posta**
lunch	*(mahn-chah)* **la mancia**
mail	**bevo**
breakfast	**mangiamo**
dinner	**vorrei**

Ecco a few more holidays which you might experience during your visit.
- ❑ **Capodanno** *(kah-poh-dahn-noh)* . . . . New Year's Day
- ❑ **Festa della Resistenza** *(fes-tah)(del-lah)(reh-zee-sten-tsah)* . . . . Liberation Day
- ❑ **Pasqua** *(pah-skwah)* . . . . Easter
- ❑ **Festa del Lavoro** *(fes-tah)(del)(lah-voh-roh)* . . . . Labor Day

(teh-leh-foh-noh) Il Telefono
telephone

Che è differente about **il telefono in Italia?** Well, **Lei** never notice such things until **Lei** want

to use them. **I telefoni** allow you to call **amici,** *(ah-mee-chee)* reserve **i biglietti di teatro, di concerto o di**

balletto, *(bahl-let-toh)* make emergency calls, check on the hours of a **museo,** *(moo-zeh-oh)* rent **una macchina e** all those

friends

other **cose** which **facciamo** *(fah-chah-moh)* on a daily basis. It also gives you a certain amount of **libertà**

we do

quando Lei può make your own **telefonate.** *(teh-leh-foh-nah-teh)*

calls

I telefoni can usually be found everywhere:

in the **ufficio postale,** on the **strada**, in the

bar, at the **stazione dei treni** and in the

lobby of **il Suo albergo.**

So, let's learn how to operate **il telefono.**

The instructions can look complicated,

but remember, some of these **parole**

Lei should be able to recognize already.

Ready? Well, before you turn the page

it would be a good idea to go back **e**

review all your numbers one more time.

To dial from the United States to most other countries **Lei** need that country's international area

code. Your **elenco** *(eh-len-koh)* **telefonico** at home should have a listing of international area codes.

telephone book

Ecco some very useful words built around the word "telefono."

- ❏ **l'operatore/ la centralinista** *(loh-peh-rah-toh-reh)/(chen-trah-lee-nee-stah)* . . . . operator
- ❏ **la cabina telefonica** *(kah-bee-nah)(teh-leh-foh-nee-kah)* . . . . public telephone booth
- ❏ **l'elenco telefonico** *(leh-len-koh)(teh-leh-foh-nee-koh)* . . . . telephone book
- ❏ **la conversazione telefonica** *(kohn-vair-sah-tsee-oh-neh)(teh-leh-foh-nee-kah)* . . . . . telephone conversation

When **Lei** leave your contact numbers with friends, family **e** business colleagues, **Lei** should include your destination's country code **e** city code whenever possible . For example,

	Country Codes		**City Codes**	
Italy	39	Rome	06
		Milan	02
		Venice	041
		Naples	081
Switzerland	41	Lugano	91

To call from one city to another city **in Italia,** you may need to go to **l'ufficio postale o** call

la centralinista in your hotel. Tell **la centralinista, "Vorrei telefonare a Chicago" o**
            operator

"Vorrei telefonare a San Francisco."

Now you try it: _____
                                    (I would like to call to . . . .)

When answering **il telefono,** pick up the receiver **e** say, " *(prohn-toh)* **Pronto! Sono** _____ ".
                                                                                                            (your name)

When saying goodbye, say "**A domani,**" or "*(ar-ree-veh-dair-chee)* **Arrivederci.**" Your turn —
                          until tomorrow   goodbye

_____
                        (Hello. This is . . .)

_____   _____
        (goodbye)   (until tomorrow)

Non forget that **Lei può** ask . . .
              can

Quanto costa una telefonata *(nel-yee) (stah-tee) (oo-nee-tee)* **negli Stati Uniti?** _____
                                    to the   United States

Quanto costa una telefonata a Firenze? _____

Ecco free telephone calls.					
☐	**in Italia:**	**polizia** *(poh-lee-tsee-ah)*	police	113	_____
		medico *(meh-dee-koh)*	doctor	113	_____
☐	**in Svizzera:**	**polizia** *(poh-lee-tsee-ah)*	police, help	117	_____
		fuoco *(fwoh-koh)*	fire brigade	118	_____

Ecco some sample sentences for **il telefono.** Write them in the blanks **sotto.**

Vorrei telefonare a Los Angeles. _____
_{to call}

Vorrei telefonare a Alitalia all'aeroporto. _____

Vorrei telefonare a un medico. _____

(mee-oh)
Il mio numero è 38-79-10-62. _____
_{my}

(kwah-leh)
Qual'è il Suo numero di telefono? _____
_{what} _{is}

Qual'è il numero di telefono dell'albergo? _____

Eva: **Pronto! Sono la signora Martini. Vorrei parlare alla Signora Rossi.**

_____

Segretaria: **Un momento, per favore. Mi scusi, ma la linea è occupata.**
_{one} _{but}

_____

Eva: **Ripeta, per piacere.**
_{repeat}

_____

Segretaria: **Mi scusi, ma la linea è occupata.**

_____

Eva: **Bene. Grazie. Arrivederci.**
_{well}

_____

(len-tah-men-teh)
Adesso Lei are ready to use any **telefono,** anywhere. Just take it **lentamente e** speak clearly.
_{slowly}

Ecco countries **Lei** may wish to call.
- ❐ **Australia** *(ah-oo-strahl-yah)* . . . . Australia _____
- ❐ **Austria** *(ah-oo-stree-ah)* . . . . Austria _____
- ❐ **Egitto** *(eh-jeet-toh)* . . . . Egypt _____
- ❐ **Inghilterra** *(een-gheel-tair-ah)* . . . . England _____

95

(meh-troh)
Il metrò a Roma è a quick and cheap way to get around, though not as extensive as the
subway
(see-steh-mah)
sistema di autobus. A Roma, e in smaller cities, **c'è sempre l'autobus,** which is slower, but
system   always
(sem-preh)

more scenic. **Lei** may also choose to go by **tassì.**
(tahs-see)

(meh-troh)
il metrò
subway

(lah-oo-toh-boos)
l'autobus
bus

(fair-mah-tah)
la fermata del metrò
stop

(poh-steh-joh)
il posteggio dei tassì
parking place

(fair-mah-tah) (del-lah-oo-toh-boos)
la fermata dell'autobus
stop

Maps displaying the various **linee e fermate sono generalmente** posted outside every
(lee-neh-eh) lines *(fair-mah-teh)* stops
(en-trah-tah)
entrata della stazione del metrò. Almost every **pianta di Roma** also has a **metrò** map.
entrance   map
(pee-ahn-tah)

Le linee are color-coded to facilitate reading just like your example on the next page. If **Lei**
lines

deve cambiare treno or transfer to an **autobus,** look for **le coincidenze** clearly marked at
must   connections
(koh-een-chee-den-tseh)

each **fermata.**

❏	**Francia** *(frahn-chah)*	. . . .	France
❏	**Germania** *(jair-mahn-yah)*	. . . .	Germany
❏	**Grecia** *(greh-chah)*	. . . .	Greece
❏	**Irlanda** *(eer-lahn-dah)*	. . . .	Ireland
❏	**Ungheria** *(oon-gair-ee-ah)*	. . . .	Hungary

Other than having foreign words, **il metrò italiano** functions just like in **New York o Londra**.

Locate your destination, select the correct line on your practice **metrò e** hop on board.

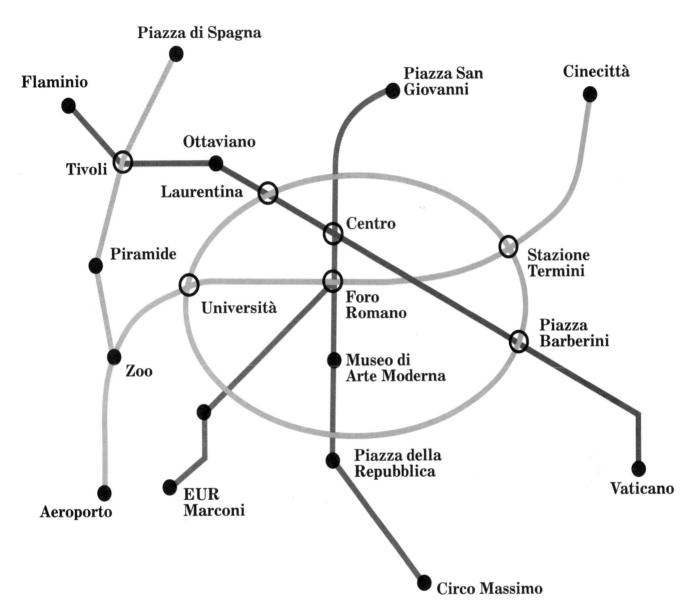

Say these questions aloud many times and don't forget you need a **biglietto** for **il metrò**.

(fair-mah-tah)
Dov'è la fermata del metrò?

Dov'è la fermata dell'autobus?

Dov'è il posteggio dei tassì?

❏	**Portogallo** *(por-toh-gahl-loh)*	Portugal
❏	**Spagna** *(spahn-yah)*	Spain
❏	**Svizzerat** *(zveet-tsair-ah)*	Switzerland
❏	**Tunisia** *(too-nee-zee-ah)*	Tunisia
❏	**Turchia** *(toor-kee-ah)*	Turkey

Practice the following basic **domande** out loud **e** then write them in the blanks below.

1. *(ohn-yee)*
   Ogni quanto c'è un metrò per il Colosseo? _____
   how often

   Ogni quanto c'è un autobus per il *(vah-tee-kah-noh)* **Vaticano?** _____

   Ogni quanto c'è un treno per l'aeroporto? _____

2. *(kwahn-doh)*
   Quando parte il treno? _____
   when

   Quando parte l'autobus? _____ *Quando parte l'autobus?* _____

3. *(kwahn-toh) (koh-stah) (beel-yet-toh)*
   Quanto costa un biglietto del metrò? _____

   Quanto costa un biglietto dell'autobus? _____

   (tah-reef-fah)
   Quanto è la tariffa? _____
   fare

4. **Dov'è la fermata del metrò?** _____

   Dov'è la fermata dell'autobus? _____

   (poh-steh-joh)
   Dov'è il posteggio dei tassì? _____

   (pohs-soh)
   Dove posso comprare un biglietto? _____
   can I

Let's change directions **e** learn **tre** new verbs. **Lei** know the basic "plug-in" formula, so

write out your own sentences using these new verbs.

(lah-vah-reh)
lavare _____
to wash

(pair-deh-reh)
perdere _____
to lose

(chee) (voo-oh-leh)
ci vuole _____
it takes

Ecco a few more holidays to keep in mind.
- ❏ **Ferragosto/Assunzione** *(fair-rah-goh-stoh/(ahs-soon-tsee-oh-neh)* .... Assumption Day
- ❏ **Ognissanti** *(ohn-yees-sahn-tee)* .... All Saints' Day
- ❏ **L'Immacolata Concezione** *(leem-mah-koh-lah-tah)(kohn-cheh-tsee-oh-neh)* ...... Immaculate Conception
- ❏ **Natale** *(nah-tah-leh)* .... Christmas

23

(ven-deh-reh) *(kohm-prah-reh)*
Vendere e Comprare
to sell   to buy

Shopping abroad is exciting. The simple everyday task of buying **un litro di latte** *(lee-troh)* **o una**
liter   milk

(meh-lah)
mela becomes a challenge that **Lei** should **adesso** be able to meet quickly **e** easily. Of course,
apple

Lei will purchase **dei** *(ree-kor-dee)* **ricordi, dei francobolli e delle cartoline** but **non** forget those many
souvenirs

(ah-spee-ree-nah)
other items ranging from shoelaces to **aspirina** that **Lei** might need unexpectedly. Locate
aspirin

your store, draw a line to it **e,** as always, write your new words in the blanks provided.

(mah-gah-tsee-noh)   *(chee-neh-mah)*
il grande magazzino _____   **il cinema** _____
department store   cinema

(loof-fee-choh) (poh-stah-leh)   *(bahn-kah)*
l'ufficio postale _____   **la banca** _____
post office   bank

(lahl-bair-goh)   *(stah-tsee-oh-neh)*
l'albergo _____   **la stazione di benzina** _____
hotel, inn   service station

99

(neh-goh-tsee) **I negozi** are generally **aperti** *(ah-pair-tee)* from
stores   open

9:00 until 18:30. Keep in mind, many shops

close for an extended lunch hour.

(mah-chel-leh-ree-ah)
la macelleria
butcher shop

_____

(lee-breh-ree-ah)
la libreria
bookstore

_____

_____ **la tintoria** *(teen-toh-ree-ah)*
dry cleaner's

_____ **l'erbivendolo** *(lair-bee-ven-doh-loh)*
greengrocer

_____ **la farmacia** *(far-mah-chee-ah)*
pharmacy, drugstore

_____ **il parcheggio** *(par-keh-joh)*
parking lot

_____ **l'edicola** *(leh-dee-koh-lah)*
newsstand

_____ **la salumeria** *(sah-loo-meh-ree-ah)*
delicatessen

_____ **sali** *(sah-lee)* **e tabacchi** *(tah-bahk-kee)*
salt   tobacco shop

Local, open-air **mercati sono** truly
(oo-neh-speh-ree-en-tsah)
un'esperienza, so be sure to check **le ore** *(oh-reh)*
experience   hours

of the one closest to **il Suo albergo.**

(lah-jen-tsee-ah) *(vee-ah-jee)*
l'agenzia di viaggi
travel agency

_____

(kweh-stoo-rah)
la questura
police station

_____

(laht-teh-ree-ah)
la latteria
dairy

(fee-oh-rah-ee-oh)
il fioraio
florist

(peh-skeh-ree-ah)
la pescheria _____
fish store

(bar)
il bar _____
serves snacks and beverages

(mair-kah-toh)
il mercato _____
market

(soo-pair-mair-kah-toh)
il supermercato _____
supermarket

(loh-roh-loh-jeh-ree-ah)
l' orologeria _____
clock and watchmaker's shop

(pah-nee-fee-choh)
il panificio ———— il panificio ————
bakery

(pah-stee-cheh-ree-ah)
la pasticceria _____
pastry shop

(lah-vahn-deh-ree-ah)
la lavanderia _____
laundromat

(kar-toh-leh-ree-ah)
la cartoleria
stationery store

(par-rook-kee-eh-reh)
il parrucchiere
hairdresser

In Italia, the ground floor is called **"il**
(pee-ahn-tair-reh-noh)
pianterreno." The first floor (**primo**

piano) **è** the next floor up **e** so on.

101

24

Il Grande Magazzino

(grahn-deh) *(mah-gah-tsee-noh)*

department store

At this point, **Lei** should just about be ready for **il Suo viaggio**. **Lei** have gone shopping for those last-minute odds 'n ends. Most likely, the store directory at your local **grande magazzino** *(mah-gah-tsee-noh)* did not look like the one **sotto**. **Lei sa che** "**bambino**" *(bahm-bee-noh)* is Italian for "<u>child</u>" so if **Lei ha bisogno di** something for a child, **Lei** would probably look on the **secondo o terzo piano, vero?**

know

4. PIANO	cristalleria vasellame da cucina alimentari verdura	servizi da tavola mobili da cucina tavola calda salumeria	chiavi ceramica porcellana frutta
3. PIANO	libri televisori mobili da bambini giocattoli	radio strumenti musicali cartoleria dischi	ristorante giornali riviste vino
2. PIANO	tutto per il bambino vestiti da donna cappelli da donna specchi	vestiti da uomo scarpe da bambino foto lampade	gabinetti antiquario tappeti mobili

1. PIANO	accessori da
	   macchina
	fazzoletti
	biancheria
		costumi da bagno
		scarpe da donna
		scarpe da uomo
			articoli sportivi
			articoli da
			   campeggio
			ferramenta

P	ombrelli biglietti di auguri cappelli da uomo gioielleria	guanti articoli di pelle e cuoio calze	cinture orologi profumeria pasticceria

Let's start a checklist **per il Suo viaggio**. Besides **vestiti, di che ha bisogno?** As you learn

(veh-stee-tee) *(keh)* *(bee-zohn-yoh)*

clothing *what do you need*

these **parole,** assemble these items **in un angolo** of your **casa**. Check **e** make sure that they

(ahn-goh-loh)

corner

sono puliti e ready **per il Suo viaggio**. Be sure to do the same **con** the rest of **le cose** that

(poo-lee-tee) *with* *things*

clean

Lei pack. On the next pages, match each item to its picture, draw a line to it and write out the word many times. As **Lei** organize these things, check them off on this list. Do not forget to take the next group of sticky labels and label these **cose oggi.**

(oh-jee)

today

(pahs-sah-por-toh)
il passaporto
passport

  ☐

(beel-yet-toh)
il biglietto
ticket

  ☐

(vah-lee-jah)
la valigia
suitcase

  ☐

(bor-sah)
la borsa
handbag

la borsa, la borsa, la borsa ✔

(por-tah-fohl-yoh)
il portafoglio
wallet

  ☐

(deh-nah-roh)
il denaro
money

  ☐

(kar-teh) (kreh-dee-toh)
le carte di credito
credit cards

  ☐

(trah-vel) (check)
i travel check
traveler's checks

  ☐

(mahk-kee-nah) (foh-toh-grah-fee-kah)
la macchina fotografica
camera

  ☐

(pel-lee-koh-lah)
la pellicola
film

  ☐

(koh-stoo-meh) (bahn-yoh)
il costume da bagno
swimsuit

  ☐

(koh-stoo-meh) (bahn-yoh)
il costume da bagno
swimsuit

  ☐

(sahn-dah-lee)
i sandali
sandals

  ☐

(ohk-kee-ah-lee) (soh-leh)
gli occhiali da sole
sunglasses

  ☐

(spah-tsoh-lee-noh) (den-tee)
lo spazzolino da denti
toothbrush

  ☐

(den-tee-free-choh)
il dentifricio
toothpaste

  ☐

(sah-poh-neh)
il sapone
soap

  ☐

(rah-zoy-oh)
il rasoio
razor

  ☐

(deh-oh-doh-rahn-teh)
il deodorante
deodorant

  ☐

(pet-tee-neh)
il pettine
comb

il pettine, il pettine ✓

(soh-prah-bee-toh)
il soprabito
overcoat

(lohm-brel-loh)
l'ombrello
umbrella

(leem-pair-meh-ah-bee-leh)
l'impermeabile
raincoat

(gwahn-tee)
i guanti
gloves

(kahp-pel-loh)
il cappello
hat

(kahp-pel-loh)
il cappello
hat

(stee-vah-lee)
gli stivali
boots

(skar-peh)
le scarpe
shoes

(skar-peh) **(ten-nees)**
le scarpe da tennis
tennis shoes

(lah-bee-toh)
l'abito
suit

(krah-vaht-tah)
la cravatta
tie

(kah-mee-chah)
la camicia
shirt

(fah-tsoh-let-toh)
il fazzoletto
handkerchief

(jahk-kah)
la giacca
jacket, blazer

(pahn-tah-loh-nee)
i pantaloni
trousers

(jeans)
i jeans
jeans

(short)
i short
shorts

(mahl-yet-tah)
la maglietta
T-shirt

(moo-tahn-deh)
le mutande
underpants

(kah-noht-tee-eh-rah)
la canottiera
undershirt

(veh-stee-toh)
il vestito
dress

(kah-mee-chet-tah)
la camicetta
blouse

(gohn-nah)
la gonna
skirt

la gonna, la gonna, la gonna ✔

(mahl-yah)
la maglia
sweater

(soht-toh-veh-steh)
la sottoveste
slip

(reh-jee-pet-toh)
il reggipetto
brassiere

(moo-tahn-deh)
le mutande
underpants

(kahl-tsee-nee)
i calzini
socks

(kahl-tseh)
le calze
pantyhose

(pee-jah-mah)
il pigiama
pajamas

(kah-mee-chah) *(noht-teh)*
la camicia da notte
nightshirt

(lahk-kahp-pah-toy-oh)
l' accappatoio
bathrobe

(pahn-toh-foh-leh)
le pantofole
slippers

(sah-poh-neh)
From now on, **Lei ha il "sapone"** e non "soap." Having assembled these **cose, Lei** are ready
have   things

viaggiare. Let's add these important shopping phrases to your basic repertoire.
to travel

(keh) *(tahl-yah)*
Che taglia? _____
what size

(mee) *(vah)*
Questo mi va. _____
this fits me

Questo non mi va. _____
this does not fit me

Treat yourself to a final review. **Lei sa** the names for **i negozi** *(neh-goh-tsee)* **italiani,** so let's practice

shopping. Just remember your key question **parole** that you learned in Step 2. Whether **Lei**

need to buy **ricordi** *(ree-kor-dee)* **o libri** the necessary **parole** are the same.
souvenirs

1.   First step — **Dove?**

Dov'è la latteria?   **Dov'è la banca?**   **Dov'è il fioraio?** *(fee-oh-rah-ee-oh)*   **Dov'è il cinema?** *(chee-neh-mah)*

_____
                    (Where is the department store?)

_____
                    (Where is the grocery store?)

_____
                    (Where is the market?)

2.   Second step — tell them what **Lei** are looking for, need **o vorrebbe.**

Ho bisogno di . . .   **Vorrei . . .**   **Lei ha . . . ?**
I need   I would like   do you have

_____
                    (Do you have postcards?)

_____
                    (I would like four stamps.)

_____
                    (I need toothpaste.)

_____
                    (I would like to buy film.)

_____
                    (Do you have coffee?)

Go through the glossary at the end of this **libro e** select **venti parole.** Drill the above patterns **con** these twenty **parole.** Don't cheat. Drill them **oggi.** *(oh-jee)* **Adesso,** take **venti** more **parole dal Suo** glossary **e** do the same.

3. Third step — find out **quanto costa.** *(kwahn-toh)*

Quanto è?	**Quanto costa un francobollo?** *(frahn-koh-bohl-loh)*	**Quanto costa una cartolina?**

_____ (How much does the toothpaste cost?)

_____ (How much does the soap cost?)

_____ (How much does a cup of tea cost?)

4. Fourth step — success! I found it!

Once **Lei** find what **Lei** would like, **Lei dice,** *(dee-cheh)*

Vorrei questo, per favore. *(kwes-toh)* _____ *say* *Vorrei questo, per favore.*
that

or

Mi dia questo, per favore. _____
give me

O if **Lei** would not like it, **Lei dice,**

Non vorrei questo, grazie. _____

or

Non mi piace. *(mee)(pee-ah-cheh)* _____
I do not like it

Congratulations! You have finished. By now you should have stuck your labels, flashed your cards, cut out your menu guide and packed your suitcases. You should be very pleased with your accomplishment. You have learned what it sometimes takes others years to achieve and you hopefully had fun doing it. **Buon viaggio!**

Glossary

This glossary contains words used in this book only. It is not meant to be a dictionary. Consider purchasing a dictionary which best suits your needs - small for traveling, large for reference, or specialized for specific vocabulary needs.

The words here are all presented in alphabetical order followed by the pronunciation guide used in this book.

Remember that Italian words can change their endings depending upon how they are used. Not all variations are given here. If you need a refresher on how to make a noun plural or how to change an adjective from masculine to feminine, refer to page 49.

A

a *(ah)* .... at, to
a domani *(ah)(doh-mah-nee)* .... until tomorrow
abbiamo *(ahb-bee-ah-moh)* .... we have
abitare *(ah-bee-tah-reh)* .... to live, to reside
abito, l' *(ah-bee-toh)* .... suit
accanto a *(ahk-kahn-toh)(ah)* .... next to
accappatoio, l' *(ahk-kahp-pah-toy-oh)* .... bathrobe
accettare *(ah-chet-tah-reh)* .... to accept
acqua, l' *(ah-kwah)* .... water
adesso *(ah-des-soh)* .... now
aereo, l' *(ah-eh-reh-oh)* .... airplane
aereoporto, l' *(ah-eh-roh-por-toh)* .... airport
agenzia di noleggio, l' *(ah-jen-tsee-ah)(dee)(noh-leh-joh)* ...
.... car rental agency
agenzia di viaggi, l' *(ah-jen-tsee-ah)(dee)(vee-ah-jee)* ....
.... travel agency
agnello, l' *(ahn-yel-loh)* .... lamb
agosto *(ah-goh-stoh)* .... August
aiuto *(eye-oo-toh)* .... help
al forno *(ahl)(for-noh)* .... baked
albergatore, l' *(ahl-bair-gah-toh-reh)* .... hotelkeeper
albergo, l' *(ahl-bair-goh)* .... hotel
alcool, l' *(ahl-kohl)* .... alcohol
alfabeto, l' *(ahl-fah-beh-toh)* .... alphabet
al *(ahl)* .... to the, at the
alla *(ahl-lah)* .... to the, at the
alla griglia *(ahl-lah)(greel-yah)* .... grilled
alle *(ahl-leh)* .... at the, at
allo *(ahl-loh)* .... to the, at the
Alpi, le *(ahl-pee)* .... Alps
alto *(ahl-toh)* .... tall
America, l' *(ah-meh-ree-kah)* .... America
americano, l' *(ah-meh-ree-kah-noh)* .... American
amico, l' *(ah-mee-koh)* .... friend
anche *(ahn-keh)* .... also
ancora *(ahn-koh-rah)* .... more, still
andare *(ahn-dah-reh)* .... to go
andare in aereo *(ahn-dah-reh)(een)(ah-eh-reh-oh)* .... to fly
andare in macchina *(ahn-dah-reh)(een)(mahk-kee-nah)* .. to drive
andata e ritorno *(ahn-dah-tah)(eh)(ree-tor-noh)* .. round-trip
angolo, l' *(ahn-goh-loh)* .... corner
animale, l' *(ah-nee-mah-leh)* .... animal
antipasti, gli *(ahn-tee-pah-stee)* .... appetizers
aperto *(ah-pair-toh)* .... open
appartamento, l' *(ahp-par-tah-men-toh)* .... apartment
appuntamenti, gli *(ahp-poon-tah-men-tee)* ... appointments
apra *(ah-prah)* .... open
aprile *(ah-pree-leh)* .... April
arancione *(ah-rahn-choh-neh)* .... orange (color)
armadietto di cucina, l' *(ar-mah-dee-et-toh)(dee)(koo-chee-nah)*
.... cupboard

armadio, l' *(ar-mah-dee-oh)* .... wardrobe
arriva *(ar-ree-vah)* .... arrive, arrives
arrivare *(ar-ree-vah-reh)* .... to arrive
arrivederci *(ar-ree-veh-dair-chee)* .... goodbye
arrivo, l' *(ah-ree-voh)* .... arrival
arrosto *(ar-roh-stoh)* .... roasted
asciugamani, gli *(ah-shoo-gah-mah-nee)* .... towels
aspettare *(ah-spet-tah-reh)* .... to wait (for)
aspirina, l' *(ah-spee-ree-nah)* .... aspirin
attenzione, l' *(aht-ten-tsee-oh-neh)* .... attention
attore, l' *(aht-toh-reh)* .... actor
Australia, l' *(ah-oo-strahl-yah)* .... Australia
Austria, l' *(ah-oo-stree-ah)* .... Austria
auto, l' *(ah-oo-toh)* .... car
autobus, l' *(ah-oo-toh-boos)* .... bus
autostrada, l' *(ah-oo-toh-strah-dah)* ...... highway, freeway
autunno, l' *(ah-oo-toon-noh)* .... autumn
avere *(ah-veh-reh)* .... to have
avere bisogno di *(ah-veh-reh)(bee-zohn-yoh)(dee)* .. to need

B

baia, la *(bah-ee-ah)* .... bay
balcone, il *(bahl-koh-neh)* .... balcony
balletto, il *(bahl-let-toh)* .... ballet
bambino, il *(bahm-bee-noh)* .... child
banana, la *(bah-nah-nah)* .... banana
banca, la *(bahn-kah)* .... bank
bar, il *(bar)* .... bar, pub
basso *(bahs-soh)* .... short
bel *(bel)* .... nice, beautiful
bella *(bel-lah)* .... nice, beautiful
bello *(bel-loh)* .... nice, beautiful
belle *(bel-leh)* .... nice, beautiful
bene *(beh-neh)* .... good, well
benedizione, la *(beh-neh-dee-tsee-oh-neh)* ...... benediction
benzina, la *(ben-tsee-nah)* .... gas
bere *(beh-reh)* .... to drink
bevande, le *(beh-vahn-deh)* .... beverages
bianco *(bee-ahn-koh)* .... white
bicchiere, il *(beek-kee-eh-reh)* .... glass
bicchiere da vino, il *(beek-kee-eh-reh)(dah)(vee-noh)* ....
.... wine glass
bicicletta, la *(bee-chee-klet-tah)* .... bicycle
biglietto, il *(beel-yet-toh)* .... bank note, bill, ticket
binario, il *(bee-nah-ree-oh)* .... train track
birra, la *(beer-rah)* .... beer
biscotto, il *(bee-skoht-toh)* .... biscuit, cookie
bisogno, il *(bee-zohn-yoh)* .... need
bistecca, la *(bee-stek-kah)* .... steak
blu *(bloo)* .... blue
bollito *(bohl-lee-toh)* .... boiled
borsa, la *(bor-sah)* .... handbag, purse

bottiglia, la *(boht-teel-yah)* .... bottle
breve *(breh-veh)* .... brief, short
brillante *(breel-lahn-teh)* .... shining, brilliant
buca delle lettere, la *(boo-kah)(del-leh)(let-teh-reh)* ... mailbox
buon, buona, buono *(bwohn)(bwoh-nah)(bwoh-noh)* ... good
   buon appetito *(bwohn)(ahp-peh-tee-toh)* .. enjoy your meal
   buon divertimento *(bwohn)(dee-vair-tee-men-toh)* .. have fun
   buona fortuna *(bwoh-nah)(for-too-nah)* .... good luck
   buon giorno *(bwohn)(jor-noh)* ... good morning, good day
   buona notte *(bwoh-nah)(noht-teh)* .... good night
   buona sera *(bwoh-nah)(seh-rah)* .... good evening
   buon viaggio *(bwohn)(vee-ah-joh)* ...... have a good trip!
burro, il *(boor-roh)* .... butter

C

cabina telefonica, la *(kah-bee-nah)(teh-leh-foh-nee-kah)* ....
.... telephone booth
cacciagione, la *(kah-chah-joh-neh)* .... wild game
caffè, il *(kahf-feh)* .... coffee
caldo *(kahl-doh)* .... warm, hot
calendario, il *(kah-len-dah-ree-oh)* .... calendar
calze, le *(kahl-tseh)* .... pantyhose
calzino, il *(kahl-tsee-noh)* .... sock
cambiare *(kahm-bee-ah-reh)* ....
.... to transfer (vehicles), to change (money)
camera, la *(kah-meh-rah)* .... room
   camera doppia, la *(kah-meh-rah)(dohp-pyah)* . double room
   camera singola, la *(kah-meh-rah)(seen-goh-lah)* single room
   camera da letto, la *(kah-meh-rah)(dah)(let-toh)* ... bedroom
cameriera, la *(kah-meh-ree-eh-rah)* .... waitress
cameriere, il *(kah-meh-ree-eh-reh)* .... waiter
camicetta, la *(kah-mee-chet-tah)* .... blouse
camicia, la *(kah-mee-chah)* .... shirt
camicia da notte, la *(kah-mee-chah)(dah)(noht-teh)* .. nightshirt
Canada, il *(kah-nah-dah)* .... Canada
canadese *(kah-nah-deh-zeh)* .... Canadian
cane, il *(kah-neh)* .... dog
canottiera, la *(kah-noht-tee-eh-rah)* .... undershirt
cantina, la *(kahn-tee-nah)* .... cellar, basement
capire *(kah-pee-reh)* .... to understand
   io capisco *(ee-oh)(kah-pee-skoh)* .... I understand
capitale, la *(kah-pee-tah-leh)* .... capital
Capodanno *(kah-poh-dahn-noh)* .... New Year's Day
cappello, il *(kahp-pel-loh)* .... hat
carne, la *(kar-neh)* .... meat
caro *(kah-roh)* .... expensive
   è troppo caro *(eh)(trohp-poh)(kah-roh)* .. (it) is too expensive
carta, la *(kar-tah)* .... paper, map
carta di credito, la *(kar-tah)(dee)(kreh-dee-toh)* ... credit card
cartoleria, la *(kar-toh-leh-ree-ah)* .... stationery store
cartolina, la *(kar-toh-lee-nah)* .... postcard
casa, la *(kah-zah)* .... house
cassa, la *(kahs-sah)* .... cashier's desk
castello, il *(kah-stel-loh)* .... castle
categoria, la *(kah-teh-goh-ree-ah)* .... category
cattedrale, la *(kaht-teh-drah-leh)* .... cathedral
cattivo *(kaht-tee-voh)* .... bad
cattolico *(kaht-toh-lee-koh)* .... Catholic
c'è *(cheh)* .... there is
cena, la *(cheh-nah)* .... dinner
Centigrado *(chen-tee-grah-doh)* .... Centigrade
cento *(chen-toh)* .... one hundred
centralinista, la *(chen-trah-lee-strah)* ... telephone operator
centro, il *(chen-troh)* .... center, downtown
ceramiche, le *(cheh-rah-mee-keh)* .... pottery
cerimonia, la *(cheh-ree-moh-nee-ah)* .... ceremony
certo *(chair-toh)* .... certainly

cestino, il *(cheh-stee-noh)* .... wastebasket
che *(keh)* .... what
chi *(kee)* .... who
chiamarsi *(kee-ah-mar-see)* .... to be called
chiesa, la *(kee-eh-zah)* .... church
chiuso *(kee-oo-zoh)* .... closed
ci sono *(chee)(soh-noh)* .... there are
ci vuole *(chee)(voo-oh-leh)* .... it takes
ciao *(chow)* .... hi!/bye!
cinema, il *(chee-neh-mah)* .... cinema, movie house
cinese, il *(chee-neh-zeh)* .... Chinese
cinquanta *(cheen-kwahn-tah)* .... fifty
cinque *(cheen-kweh)* .... five
cinquecento *(cheen-kweh-chen-toh)* .... five hundred
cioccolato, il *(chohk-koh-lah-toh)* .... chocolate
coincidenza, la *(koh-een-chee-den-tsah)* ... train connection
colazione, la *(koh-lah-tsee-oh-neh)* .... breakfast, lunch
colore, il *(koh-loh-reh)* .... color
coltello, il *(kohl-tel-loh)* .... knife
come *(koh-meh)* .... how
   Come va? *(koh-meh)(vah)* .... How are you?
comincia *(koh-meen-chah)* .... commences, begins
comprare *(kohm-prah-reh)* .... to buy
computer, il *(kohm-pyoo-tair)* .... computer
comunicazione, la *(koh-moo-nee-kah-tsee-oh-neh)* ....
.... communication
con *(kohn)* .... with
concerto, il *(kohn-chair-toh)* .... concert
conservazione, la *(kohn-sair-vah-tsee-oh-neh)* .. conservation
continui *(kohn-tee-noo-ee)* .... continue
conto, il *(kohn-toh)* .... bill
conversazione, la *(kohn-vair-sah-tsee-oh-neh)* .. conversation
coperta, la *(koh-pair-tah)* .... blanket
coraggio, il *(koh-rah-joh)* .... courage
corretto *(kor-ret-toh)* .... correct
corto *(kor-toh)* .... short
cosa, la *(koh-zah)* .... thing
costa *(koh-stah)* .... (it) costs
costare *(koh-stah-reh)* .... to cost
costume, il *(koh-stoo-meh)* .... custom
costume da bagno, il *(koh-stoo-meh)(dah)(bahn-yoh)* ......
.... swimsuit
cotto *(koht-toh)* .... cooked
cravatta, la *(krah-vaht-tah)* .... tie
cucchiaio, il *(kook-kee-eye-oh)* .... spoon
cucina, la *(koo-chee-nah)* .... kitchen, stove
cugina, la *(koo-jee-nah)* .... female cousin
cugino, il *(koo-jee-noh)* .... male cousin
cuscino, il *(koo-shee-noh)* .... pillow

D

da *(dah)* .... of, from
dagli *(dahl-yee)* .... from the
dal *(dahl)* .... from the
dalla *(dahl-lah)* .... from the
danza, la *(dahn-tsah)* .... dance
davanti a *(dah-vahn-tee)(ah)* .... in front of
decorato *(deh-koh-rah-toh)* .... decorated
degli *(del-yee)* .... some, of the
dei *(deh-ee)* .... some, of the
del, della, delle *(del)(del-lah)(del-leh)* .... some, of the
delizioso *(deh-lee-tsee-oh-zoh)* .... delicious
denaro, il *(deh-nah-roh)* .... money
denso *(den-soh)* .... dense
dentifricio, il *(den-tee-free-choh)* .... toothpaste
deodorante, il *(deh-oh-doh-rahn-teh)* .... deodorant

deposito bagagli, il *(deh-poh-zee-toh)(bah-gahl-yee)* . . . . left-luggage office
desiderio, il *(deh-zee-deh-ree-oh)* . . . . desire, wish
destra *(deh-strah)* . . . . right
deviazione, la *(deh-vee-ah-tsee-oh-neh)* . . . . detour
di *(dee)* . . . . of, in
dicembre *(dee-chem-breh)* . . . . December
diciannove *(dee-chahn-noh-veh)* . . . . nineteen
diciassette *(dee-chahs-set-teh)* . . . . seventeen
diciotto *(dee-choht-toh)* . . . . eighteen
dieci *(dee-eh-chee)* . . . . ten
dietro *(dee-eh-troh)* . . . . behind
difficile *(dee-fee-chee-leh)* . . . . difficult
dire *(dee-reh)* . . . . to say
si dice *(see)(dee-cheh)* . . . . one says
diretto *(dee-ret-toh)* . . . . direct
direzione, la *(dee-reh-tsee-oh-neh)* . . . . direction
diritto *(dee-reet-toh)* . . . . straight ahead
disastro, il *(dee-zah-stroh)* . . . . accident, disaster
disco di sosta, il *(dee-skoh)(dee)(soh-stah)* . . . . parking disk
distanza, la *(dee-stahn-tsah)* . . . . distance
divertimento, il *(dee-vair-tee-men-toh)* . . . . fun
divino *(dee-vee-noh)* . . . . divine
dizionario, il *(dee-tsee-oh-nah-ree-oh)* . . . . dictionary
doccia, la *(doh-chah)* . . . . shower
dodici *(doh-dee-chee)* . . . . twelve
dogana, la *(doh-gah-nah)* . . . . customs
dolce, il *(dohl-cheh)* . . . . pastry, sweet
dollaro, il *(dohl-lah-roh)* . . . . dollar
domanda, la *(doh-mahn-dah)* . . . . question
domani *(doh-mah-nee)* . . . . tomorrow
domenica *(doh-meh-nee-kah)* . . . . Sunday
dormire *(dor-mee-reh)* . . . . to sleep
dottore, il *(doht-toh-reh)* . . . . doctor
dove *(doh-veh)* . . . . where
dov'è *(doh-veh)* . . . . where is
dovere *(doh-veh-reh)* . . . . to have to, must, to owe
dubbio, il *(doob-bee-oh)* . . . . doubt
due *(doo-eh)* . . . . two
durante *(doo-rahn-teh)* . . . . during

E

e *(eh)* . . . . and
e mezzo *(eh)(med-zoh)* . . . . half past
e un quarto *(eh)(oon)(kwar-toh)* . . . . a quarter past
è *(eh)* . . . . (it) is
ebreo *(eh-breh-oh)* . . . . Jewish
eccellente *(eh-chel-len-teh)* . . . . excellent
ecco *(ek-koh)* . . . . here is, here are
economia, l' *(eh-koh-noh-mee-ah)* . . . . economy
economico *(eh-koh-noh-mee-koh)* . . . . inexpensive
edicola, l' *(eh-dee-koh-lah)* . . . . newsstand
Egitto, l' *(eh-jeet-toh)* . . . . Egypt
elenco telefonico, l' *(eh-len-koh)(teh-leh-foh-nee-koh)* . . . . . .
. . . . telephone book
entrare *(en-trah-reh)* . . . . to enter
entrata, l' *(en-trah-tah)* . . . . entrance
entrata principale, l' *(en-trah-tah)(preen-chee-pah-leh)* . . .
. . . . main entrance
era *(eh-rah)* . . . . was
erbivendolo, l' *(air-bee-ven-doh-loh)* . . . . greengrocer
esempio, l' *(eh-zem-pee-oh)* . . . . example
esperienza, la *(eh-speh-ree-en-tsah)* . . . . experience
est, l' *(est)* . . . . east
estate, l' *(eh-stah-teh)* . . . . summer
Europa, l' *(eh-oo-roh-pah)* . . . . Europe
europeo *(eh-oo-roh-peh-oh)* . . . . European

F

facchino, il *(fahk-kee-noh)* . . . . porter
Fahrenheit *(fah-ren-heit)* . . . . Fahrenheit
fame, la *(fah-meh)* . . . . hunger
famiglia, la *(fah-meel-yah)* . . . . family
famoso *(fah-moh-zoh)* . . . . famous
farcito *(far-chee-toh)* . . . . stuffed
fare *(fah-reh)* . . . . to do, to make
faccio *(fah-choh)* . . . . I make
fare la valigie *(fah-reh)(leh)(vah-lee-jeh)* . . . . to pack
farmacia, la *(far-mah-chee-ah)* . . . . pharmacy, drugstore
favore, il *(fah-voh-reh)* . . . . favor
fax, il *(fahx)* . . . . fax
fazzoletto, il *(fah-tsoh-let-toh)* . . . . handkerchief
febbraio *(feb-bry-oh)* . . . . February
fede, la *(feh-deh)* . . . . faith
fermata, la *(fair-mah-tah)* . . . . stop
Festa del Lavoro *(fes-tah)(del)(lah-voh-roh)* . . . . Labor Day
Festa della Resistenza *(fes-tah)(del-lah)(reh-zee-sten-tsah)* . . .
. . . . Liberation Day
figli, i *(feel-yee)* . . . . children
figlia, la *(feel-yah)* . . . . daughter
figlio, il *(feel-yoh)* . . . . son
film, il *(feelm)* . . . . film
filtro, il *(feel-troh)* . . . . filter
finalmente *(fee-nahl-men-teh)* . . . . finally
fine, la *(fee-neh)* . . . . end
finestra, la *(fee-neh-strah)* . . . . window
finito *(fee-nee-toh)* . . . . finished, ended
fioraio, il *(fee-oh-rah-ee-oh)* . . . . florist
fiore, il *(fee-oh-reh)* . . . . flower
fontana, la *(fohn-tah-nah)* . . . . fountain
forchetta, la *(for-ket-tah)* . . . . fork
foresta, la *(foh-reh-stah)* . . . . forest
forma, la *(for-mah)* . . . . form
formaggio, il *(for-mah-joh)* . . . . cheese
fra *(frah)* . . . . between
francese, il *(frahn-cheh-zeh)* . . . . French
Francia, la *(frahn-chah)* . . . . France
francobollo, il *(frahn-koh-bohl-loh)* . . . . stamp
fratello, il *(frah-tel-loh)* . . . . brother
freddo *(fred-doh)* . . . . cold
fresco *(freh-skoh)* . . . . cool, fresh
frigorifero, il *(free-goh-ree-feh-roh)* . . . . refrigerator
fritto *(freet-toh)* . . . . fried
frutta, la *(froot-tah)* . . . . fruit
fumare *(foo-mah-reh)* . . . . to smoke
fuoco, il *(fwoh-koh)* . . . . fire, fire brigade

G

gabinetto, il *(gah-bee-net-toh)* . . . . lavatory, restroom
galleria, la *(gahl-leh-ree-ah)* . . . . gallery, tunnel
garage, il *(gah-rahzh)* . . . . garage
gatto, il *(gaht-toh)* . . . . cat
generalmente *(jeh-neh-rahl-men-teh)* . . . . generally
genitori, i *(jeh-nee-toh-ree)* . . . . parents
gennaio *(jen-ny-oh)* . . . . January
gentile *(jen-tee-leh)* . . . . kind, gentle
geografia, la *(jeh-oh-grah-fee-ah)* . . . . geography
geometria, la *(jeh-oh-meh-tree-ah)* . . . . geometry
Germania, la *(jair-mahn-yah)* . . . . Germany
giacca, la *(jahk-kah)* . . . . jacket
giallo *(jahl-loh)* . . . . yellow
Giappone, il *(jahp-poh-neh)* . . . . Japan
giardino, il *(jar-dee-noh)* . . . . garden

gioielli, i (joy-el-lee) . . . . jewelry
giornale, il (jor-nah-leh) . . . . newspaper
giorno, il, (jor-noh) . . . . day
giovane (joh-vah-neh) . . . . young
giovedì (joh-veh-dee) . . . . Thursday
giri (jee-ree) . . . . turn
giugno (joon-yoh) . . . . June
gli (l-yee) . . . . the
gondola, la (gohn-doh-lah) . . . . Venetian boat
gonna, la (gohn-nah) . . . . skirt
governo, il (goh-vair-noh) . . . . government
grado, il (grah-doh) . . . . degree
grande (grahn-deh) . . . . grand, big, large
grande magazzino, il (grahn-deh)(mah-gah-tsee-noh) . . . . . .
. . . . department store
grazie (grah-tsee-eh) . . . . thank you
Grecia, la (greh-chah) . . . . Greece
grigio (gree-joh) . . . . gray
guanto, il (gwahn-toh) . . . . glove
guida, la (gwee-dah) . . . . guide
guidare (gwee-dah-reh) . . . . to drive

H

ha (ah) . . . . (he, she, it) has
ho (oh) . . . . I have
ho fame (oh)(fah-meh) . . . . I'm hungry
ho perso il mio (oh)(pair-soh)(eel)(mee-oh) I have lost my
ho sete (oh)(seh-teh) . . . . I'm thirsty

I

i (ee) . . . . the (plural)
idea, l' (ee-deh-ah) . . . . idea
ieri (ee-eh-ree) . . . . yesterday
il (eel) . . . . the (singular)
Immacolata Concezione (eem-mah-koh-lah-tah)(kohn-cheh-
tsee-oh-neh) . . . . Immaculate Conception
imparare (eem-pah-rah-reh) . . . . to learn
impermeabile, l' (eem-pair-meh-ah-bee-leh) . . . . . . raincoat
importante (eem-por-tahn-teh) . . . . important
in (een) . . . . in, into
incantevole (een-kahn-teh-vol-leh) . . . enchanting, charming
indirizzo, l' (een-dee-ree-tsoh) . . . . address
indispensabile (een-dee-spen-sah-bee-leh) . . . indispensable
individuo, l' (een-dee-vee-doo-oh) . . . . individual
industria, l' (een-doo-stree-ah) . . . . industry
industrioso (een-doo-stree-oh-zoh) . . . . industrious
influenza, l' (een-floo-en-tsah) . . . . influence
informazione, l' (een-for-mah-tsee-oh-neh) . . . . . information
ingegnere, l' (een-jen-yeh-reh) . . . . engineer
Inghilterra, l' (een-gheel-tair-rah) . . . . England
inglese (een-gleh-zeh) . . . . English
ingresso, l' (een-gres-soh) . . . . entrance
innamorato (een-nah-moh-rah-toh) . . . . enamored, in love
insalata, l' (een-sah-lah-tah) . . . . salad
interamente (een-teh-rah-men-teh) . . . . entirely
interessante (een-teh-res-sahn-teh) . . . . interesting
internazionale (een-tair-nah-tsee-oh-nah-leh) . . international
inverno, l' (een-vair-noh) . . . . winter
invito, l' (een-vee-toh) . . . . invitation
io (ee-oh) I
io sono (ee-oh)(soh-noh) . . . . I am
Irlanda, l' (eer-lahn-dah) . . . . Ireland
Israele, l' (eez-rah-eh-leh) . . . . Israel
Italia, l' (ee-tahl-yah) . . . . Italy
Italiani, gli (ee-tahl-yah-nee) . . . . Italians
italiano (ee-tahl-yah-noh) . . . . Italian

J

jeans, i (jeans) . . . . jeans

L

l' (l) . . . . the (singular)
la (lah) . . . . the (singular)
lago, il (lah-goh) . . . . lake
lampada, la (lahm-pah-dah) . . . . lamp
largo (lar-goh) . . . . wide, broad
latte, il (laht-teh) . . . . milk
latteria, la (laht-teh-ree-ah) . . . . dairy
lavanderia, la (lah-vahn-deh-ree-ah) . . . . laundry
lavandino, il (lah-vahn-dee-noh) . . . . sink
lavare (lah-vah-reh) . . . . to wash
le (leh) . . . . the (plural)
leggere (leh-jeh-reh) . . . . to read
legume, il (leh-goo-meh) . . . . vegetable
lei (leh-ee) . . . . she
Lei (leh-ee) . . . . you (singular)
lentamente (len-tah-men-teh) . . . . slowly
lento (len-toh) . . . . slow
lettera, la (let-teh-rah) . . . . letter
letto, il (let-toh) . . . . bed
lezione, la (leh-tsee-oh-neh) . . . . lesson, lecture
lì (lee) . . . . there
libero (lee-beh-roh) . . . . free, liberated
libertà, la (lee-bair-tah) . . . . liberty
libreria, la (lee-breh-ree-ah) . . . . bookstore
libro, il (lee-broh) . . . . book
linea, la (lee-neh-ah) . . . . line
lingua, la (leen-gwah) . . . . language
lira, la (lee-rah) . . . . Italian unit of currency
lista, la (lee-stah) . . . . list, menu
litro, il (lee-troh) . . . . liter
lo (loh) . . . . it, the (singular)
locale (loh-kah-leh) . . . . local
loro (loh-roh) . . . . they, their
lotteria, la (loht-teh-ree-ah) . . . . lottery
luglio (lool-yoh) . . . . July
lui (loo-ee) . . . . he, him
lunedì (loo-neh-dee) . . . . Monday
lungo (loon-goh) . . . . long

M

macchina, la (mahk-kee-nah) . . . . car
macchina da noleggiare, la (mahk-kee-nah)(dah)(noh-leh-
jah-reh) . . . . rental car
macchina fotografica, la (mahk-kee-nah)(foh-toh-grah-fee-kah)
. . . . camera
macelleria, la (mah-chel-leh-ree-ah) . . . . butcher shop
madre, la (mah-dreh) . . . . mother
maestro, il (mah-eh-stroh) . . . . master, teacher
maggio (mah-joh) . . . . May
maglia, la (mahl-yah) . . . . sweater
maglietta, la (mahl-yet-tah) . . . . T-shirt
magnifico (mahn-yee-fee-koh) . . . . magnificent
maiale, il (my-ah-leh) . . . . pork
malato (mah-lah-toh) . . . . sick
male (mah-leh) . . . . bad
mancia, la (mahn-chah) . . . . tip
mandare (mahn-dah-reh) . . . . to send
mangiare (mahn-jah-reh) . . . . to eat
maniera, la (mah-nee-eh-rah) . . . . manner, way
manzo, il (mahn-tsoh) . . . . beef
marciapiede, il (mar-chah-pee-eh-deh) . . . railway platform

mare, il (mah-reh) . . . . sea
marrone (mar-roh-neh) . . . . brown
marzo (mar-tsoh) . . . . March
martedì (mar-teh-dee) . . . . Tuesday
matita, la (mah-tee-tah) . . . . pencil
matrimonio, il (mah-tree-moh-nee-oh) . . . marriage, wedding
mattina, la (maht-tee-nah) . . . . morning
medico, il (meh-dee-koh) . . . . physician
mela, la (meh-lah) . . . . apple
memoria, la (meh-moh-ree-ah) . . . . memory
meno (meh-noh) . . . . less, minus
   meno un quarto (meh-noh)(oon)(kwar-toh) . . . a quarter to
menù, il (meh-noo) . . . . menu
meraviglioso (meh-rah-veel-yoh-zoh) . . . . marvelous
mercato, il (mair-kah-toh) . . . . market
mercoledì (mair-koh-leh-dee) . . . . Wednesday
mese, il, (meh-zeh) . . . . month
metallo, il (meh-tahl-loh) . . . . metal
metro, il (meh-troh) . . . . meter
metrò, il (meh-troh) . . . . subway
mezzanotte, la (med-zah-noht-teh) . . . . midnight
mezzo (med-zoh) . . . . middle
mezzogiorno, il (med-zoh-jor-noh) . . . . noon
mi chiamo (mee)(kee-ah-moh) . . . . my name is
mi dia (mee)(dee-ah) . . . . give me
mi dispiace (mee)(dee-spee-ah-cheh) . . . . I'm sorry
mi scriva (mee)(skree-vah) . . . . write for me
mi scusi (mee)(skoo-zee) . . . . excuse me
mi sono perso (mee)(soh-noh)(pair-soh) . . . . I'm lost
mila (mee-lah) . . . . thousand (two or more)
milione (meel-yoh-neh) . . . . million
mille (meel-leh) . . . . one thousand
minestra, la (mee-neh-strah) . . . . soup
minuto, il (mee-noo-toh) . . . . minute
mio (mee-oh) . . . . my
misura, la (mee-zoo-rah) . . . . measure, size
moda, la (moh-dah) . . . . style, fashion
molto (mohl-toh) . . . . very, a lot
momento, il (moh-men-toh) . . . . moment
moneta, la (moh-neh-tah) . . . . coin
montagna, la (mohn-tahn-yah) . . . . mountain
montone, il (mohn-toh-neh) . . . . mutton
motocicletta, la (moh-toh-chee-klet-tah) . . . . motorcycle
motore, il (moh-toh-reh) . . . . motor, engine
multicolore (mool-tee-koh-loh-reh) . . . . multi-colored
museo, il (moo-zeh-oh) . . . . museum
musica, la (moo-zee-kah) . . . . music
mutande, le (moo-tahn-deh) . . . . underpants

N

Natale (nah-tah-leh) . . . . Christmas
nativo (nah-tee-voh) . . . . native
naturale (nah-too-rah-leh) . . . . natural
nave, la (nah-veh) . . . . ship
nazionale (nah-tsee-oh-nah-leh) . . . . national
nazione, la (nah-tsee-oh-neh) . . . . nation, country
necessario (neh-ches-sah-ree-oh) . . . . necessary
negozio, il (neh-goh-tsee-oh) . . . . store
nel, nella (nel)(nel-lah) . . . . in the
nero (neh-roh) . . . . black
nevica (neh-vee-kah) . . . . it snows
niente (nee-en-teh) . . . . nothing
no (noh) . . . . no
noi (noy) . . . . we
nome, il (noh-meh) . . . . name
non (nohn) . . . . not, no

non me piace (nohn)(mee)(pee-ah-cheh) . . I do not like it
nonna, la (nohn-nah) . . . . grandmother
nonno, il (nohn-noh) . . . . grandfather
nord, il (nord) . . . . north
normale (nor-mah-leh) . . . . normal
notizia, la (noh-tee-tsee-ah) . . . . news, notice
notte, la (noht-teh) . . . . night
novanta (noh-vahn-tah) . . . . ninety
nove (noh-veh) . . . . nine
novembre (noh-vem-breh) . . . . November
numero, il (noo-meh-roh) . . . . number
nuovo (noo-oh-voh) . . . . new

O

o (oh) . . . . or
occasione, l' (ohk-kah-zee-oh-neh) . . . occasion, opportunity
occhiali, gli (ohk-kee-ah-lee) . . . . eyeglasses
occhiali da sole, gli (ohk-kee-ah-lee)(dah)(soh-leh) . . sunglasses
occupato (ohk-koo-pah-toh) . . . . occupied
odore, l' (oh-doh-reh) . . . . odor (smell)
oggetto, l' (oh-jet-toh) . . . . object
oggi (oh-jee) . . . . today
ogni (ohn-yee) . . . . each, every
ogni quanto (ohn-yee)(kwahn-toh) . . . . how often
Ognissanti (ohn-yees-sahn-tee) . . . . All Saints' Day
ombrello, l' (ohm-brel-loh) . . . . umbrella
opera, l' (oh-peh-rah) . . . . opera
operatore, l' (oh-peh-rah-toh-reh) . . . . . . telephone operator
ora, la (oh-rah) . . . . hour
orario, l' (oh-rah-ree-oh) . . . . timetable
ordinare (or-dee-nah-reh) . . . . to order
ordinario (or-dee-nah-ree-oh) . . . . ordinary
orologeria, l' (oh-roh-loh-jeh-ree-ah) . . . .
. . . . clock and watchmaker's shop
orologio, l' (oh-roh-loh-joh) . . . . clock
ospedale, l' (oh-speh-dah-leh) . . . . hospital
osteria, l' (oh-steh-ree-ah) . . . . cafe
ottanta (oht-tahn-tah) . . . . eighty
otto (oht-toh) . . . . eight
ottobre (oht-toh-breh) . . . . October
ovest, l' (oh-vest) . . . . west

P

pacco, il (pahk-koh) . . . . package
padre, il (pah-dreh) . . . . father
pagare (pah-gah-reh) . . . . to pay
pagina, la (pah-jee-nah) . . . . page
paio, il (pie-yoh) . . . . pair
palazzo, il (pah-lah-tsoh) . . . . palace
pane, il (pah-neh) . . . . bread
panificio, il (pah-nee-fee-choh) . . . . bakery
pantofole, le (pahn-toh-foh-leh) . . . . slippers
pantaloni, i (pahn-tah-loh-nee) . . . . trousers
Papa, il (pah-pah) . . . . Pope
parcheggio, il (par-keh-joh) . . . . parking lot
parchimetro, il (par-kee-meh-troh) . . . . parking meter
parco, il (par-koh) . . . . park
parenti, i (pah-ren-tee) . . . . relatives
parlare (par-lah-reh) . . . . to speak
parola, la (pah-roh-lah) . . . . word
parole crociate, le (pah-roh-leh)(kroh-chah-teh) . . . .
. . . . crossword puzzle
parrucchiere, il (par-rook-kee-eh-reh) . . . . hairdresser
parte, la (par-teh) . . . . part, portion
partenza, la (par-ten-tsah) . . . . departure
partire (par-tee-reh) . . . . to leave, to depart

Pasqua *(pah-skwah)* . . . . Easter
passaporto, il *(pahs-sah-por-toh)* . . . . passport
pasta, la *(pah-stah)* . . . . pasta
pastasciutta, la *(pah-stah-shoot-tah)* . . . . pasta
pasticceria, la *(pah-stee-cheh-ree-ah)* . . . . pastry shop
pasto, il *(pah-stoh)* . . . . meal
patata, la *(pah-tah-tah)* . . . . potato
pellicola, la *(pel-lee-koh-lah)* . . . . film
pelletteria, la *(pel-let-tair-ee-ah)* . . . . leather goods
penna, la *(pen-nah)* . . . . pen
pepe, il *(peh-peh)* . . . . pepper
per *(pair)* . . . . for
  per favore *(pair)(fah-voh-reh)* . . . . please
  per piacere *(pair)(pee-ah-cheh-reh)* . . please, if you please
perchè *(pair-keh)* . . . . why
perdere *(pair-deh-reh)* . . . . to lose
perfetto *(pair-fet-toh)* . . . . perfect
periodo, il *(peh-ree-oh-doh)* . . . . period
permanenza, la *(pair-mah-nen-tsah)* . . . . . stay, permanence
permesso, il *(pair-mes-soh)* . . . . permission
persona, la *(pair-soh-nah)* . . . . person
pesce, il *(peh-sheh)* . . . . fish
pescheria, la *(peh-skeh-ree-ah)* . . . . fish store
pettine, il *(pet-tee-neh)* . . . . comb
pezzo, il *(peh-tsoh)* . . . . piece
piacere, il *(pee-ah-cheh-reh)* . . . . pleasure
  Molto piacere *(mohl-toh)(pee-ah-cheh-reh)* . . . .
    . . . . It's a pleasure to meet you.
piano, il *(pee-ahn-oh)* . . . . floor
pianta, la *(pee-ahn-tah)* . . . . map
pianterreno, il *(pee-ahn-tair-reh-noh)* . . . . ground floor
piatto, il *(pee-aht-toh)* . . . . plate, dish
  piatto del giorno, il *(pee-aht-toh)(del)(jor-noh)* . . daily special
piazza, la *(pee-ah-tsah)* . . . . plaza, town square
piccolo *(peek-koh-loh)* . . . . little
pigiama, il *(pee-jah-mah)* . . . . pajamas
pillola, la *(peel-loh-lah)* . . . . pill
piove *(pee-oh-veh)* . . . . it rains
pittoresco *(peet-toh-reh-skoh)* . . . . picturesque
poco *(poh-koh)* . . . . a little
poi *(poy)* . . . . then
polizia, la *(poh-lee-tsee-ah)* . . . . police
pollame, il *(pohl-lah-meh)* . . . . poultry
pomeriggio, il *(poh-meh-ree-joh)* . . . . afternoon
ponte, il *(pohn-teh)* . . . . bridge
porta, la *(por-tah)* . . . . door
portafoglio, il *(por-tah-fohl-yoh)* . . . . wallet
porto, il *(por-toh)* . . . . port
Portogallo, il *(por-toh-gahl-loh)* . . . . Portugal
porzione, la *(por-tsee-oh-neh)* . . . . portion
possibile *(pohs-see-bee-leh)* . . . . possible
posta, la *(poh-stah)* . . . . mail, post office
posteggio, il *(poh-steh-joh)* . . . . parking place
posto, il *(poh-stoh)* . . . . seat
potere *(poh-teh-reh)* . . . . to be able to, can
povero *(poh-veh-roh)* . . . . poor
pranzo, il *(prahn-tsoh)* . . . . lunch
precedente *(preh-cheh-den-teh)* . . . . preceding
preciso *(preh-chee-zoh)* . . . . precise, exact
prego *(preh-goh)* . . . . you're welcome
prenotare *(preh-noh-tah-reh)* . . . . to reserve, to book
prenotazione, la *(preh-noh-tah-tsee-oh-neh)* . . . reservation
preposizione, la *(preh-poh-zee-tsee-oh-neh)* . . . . preposition
presente *(preh-zen-teh)* . . . . present
prezioso *(preh-tsee-oh-zoh)* . . . . precious, valuable

prezzo, il *(preh-tsoh)* . . . . price
prima colazione, la *(pree-mah)(koh-lah-tsee-oh-neh)* . . breakfast
primavera, la *(pree-mah-veh-rah)* . . . . spring
problema, il *(proh-bleh-mah)* . . . . problem
profumi, i *(proh-foo-mee)* . . . . perfume
pronto *(prohn-toh)* . . . . prompt, ready
  Pronto! . . . . Hello! (when answering telephone)
protestante *(proh-teh-stahn-teh)* . . . . Protestant
puliti *(poo-lee-tee)* . . . . clean

Q

quadro, il *(kwah-droh)* . . . . picture
qual *(kwahl)* . . . . what, which
qualifica, la *(kwah-lee-fee-kah)* . . . . qualification
qualità, la *(kwah-lee-tah)* . . . . quality
quando *(kwahn-doh)* . . . . when
quanti *(kwahn-tee)* . . . . how many
quantità, la *(kwahn-tee-tah)* . . . . quantity
quanto *(kwahn-toh)* . . . . how much
  Quanto costa? *(kwahn-toh)(koh-stah)* . . . .
    . . . . How much does it cost?
quaranta *(kwah-rahn-tah)* . . . . forty
quartiere, il *(kwar-tee-eh-reh)* . . . . quarter, district
quarto, un *(kwar-toh)* . . . . quarter, fourth
  e un quarto *(eh)(oon)(kwar-toh)* . . . . a quarter past
quattordici *(kwaht-tor-dee-chee)* . . . . fourteen
quattro *(kwaht-troh)* . . . . four
quattrocento *(kwaht-troh-chen-toh)* . . . . four hundred
quello *(kwel-loh)* . . . . that
questo *(kwes-toh)* . . . . this
questo mi va *(kwes-toh)(mee)(vah)* . . . . this fits me
questura, la *(kweh-stoo-rah)* . . . . police station
qui *(kwee)* . . . . here
quindici *(kween-dee-chee)* . . . . fifteen

R

radio, la *(rah-dee-oh)* . . . . radio
ragazza, la *(rah-gah-tsah)* . . . . girl
ragazzo, il *(rah-gah-tsoh)* . . . . boy
ragione, la *(rah-joh-neh)* . . . . reason
rapido *(rah-pee-doh)* . . . . rapid, fast
rasoio, il *(rah-zoy-oh)* . . . . razor
recente *(reh-chen-teh)* . . . . recent
reggipetto, il *(reh-jee-pet-toh)* . . . . brassière
religione, la *(reh-lee-joh-neh)* . . . . religion
resto, il *(reh-stoh)* . . . . rest, change (money)
ricco *(reek-koh)* . . . . rich
ricetta, la *(ree-chet-tah)* . . . . recipe
ricordo, il *(ree-kor-doh)* . . . . souvenir, record
Rinascimento, il *(ree-nah-shee-men-toh)* . . . . . Renaissance
ripeta *(ree-peh-tah)* . . . . repeat
ripetere *(ree-peh-teh-reh)* . . . . to repeat
riso, il *(ree-zoh)* . . . . rice
rispetto, il *(ree-spet-toh)* . . . . respect
risposta, la *(ree-spoh-stah)* . . . . answer
ristorante, il *(ree-stoh-rahn-teh)* . . . . restaurant
ritardo *(ree-tar-doh)* . . . . late
rivista, la *(ree-vee-stah)* . . . . magazine
Roma *(roh-mah)* . . . . Rome
rosa *(roh-zah)* . . . . pink
rosa, la *(roh-zah)* . . . . rose
rosso *(rohs-soh)* . . . . red
Russia, la *(roo-see-ah)* . . . . Russia
russo, il *(roos-soh)* . . . . Russian

113

S

sabato (sah-bah-toh) . . . . Saturday
sacco, il (sahk-koh) . . . . sack, bag
sala d'aspetto, la (sah-lah)(dah-spet-toh) . . . . waiting room
sala da pranzo, la (sah-lah)(dah)(prahn-tsoh) . . . dining room
sale, il (sah-leh) . . . . salt
salotto, il (sah-loht-toh) . . . . living room
salsa, la (sahl-sah) . . . . sauce
salumeria, la (sah-loo-meh-ree-ah) . . . . delicatessen
salute, la (sah-loo-teh) . . . . health
   in buona salute (een)(bwoh-nah)(sah-loo-teh) . . . . healthy
saluto, il (sah-loo-toh) . . . . greeting, salutation
sandali, i (sahn-dah-lee) . . . . sandals
sapere (sah-peh-reh) . . . . to know (a fact)
sapone, il (sah-poh-neh) . . . . soap
scala, la (skah-lah) . . . . staircase, stairs
   La Scala (skah-lah) . . . . opera house in Milan
scarpe, le (skar-peh) . . . . shoes
scarpe da tennis, le (skar-peh)(dah)(ten-nees) . . tennis shoes
scavo, lo (skah-voh) . . . . excavation
scena, la (sheh-nah) . . . . scene
scienza, la (shee-en-zah) . . . . science
scrivania, la (skree-vah-nee-ah) . . . . desk
scrivere (skree-veh-reh) . . . . to write
scuola, la (skoo-oh-lah) . . . . school
secondo (seh-kohn-doh) . . . . second (as in first and second)
secondo, il (seh-kohn-doh) . . . . second (time)
sedia, la (seh-dee-ah) . . . . chair
sedici (seh-dee-chee) . . . . sixteen
seduto (seh-doo-tah) . . . . seated
segnale, il (sen-yah-leh) . . . . signal, sign
segretario, il (seh-greh-tah-ree-oh) . . . . . . secretary (male)
seguente (seh-gwen-teh) . . . . following
sei (seh-ee) . . . . six
selezione, la (seh-leh-tsee-oh-neh) . . . . selection, choice
semisfera, la (seh-mee-sfeh-rah) . . . . hemisphere
semplice (sem-plee-cheh) . . . . simple, easy, one-way (ticket)
sempre (sem-preh) . . . . always
sentimento, il (sen-tee-men-toh) . . . . feeling
senza (sen-zah) . . . . without
sera, la (seh-rah) . . . . evening
serio (seh-ree-oh) . . . . serious
servizio, il (sair-vee-tsee-oh) . . . . service
sessanta (ses-sahn-tah) . . . . sixty
settanta (set-tahn-tah) . . . . seventy
sette (set-teh) . . . . seven
settembre (set-tem-breh) . . . . September
settimana, la (set-tee-mah-nah) . . . . week
sfortunato (sfor-too-nah-toh) . . . . unfortunate, unlucky
short, i (short) . . . . shorts
sì (see) . . . . yes
Sicilia (see-chee-lee-ah) . . . . Sicily
sicuro (see-koo-roh) . . . . safe, sure, secure
sidro, il (see-droh) . . . . cider
sigaretta, la (see-gah-ret-tah) . . . . cigarette
sigaro, il (see-gah-roh) . . . . cigar
signor, il (seen-yor) . . . . Mr.
signora, la (seen-yoh-rah) . . . . lady, woman, Mrs.
signore, il (seen-yoh-reh) . . . . man
signorina, la (seen-yoh-ree-nah) . . . . Miss
simile (see-mee-leh) . . . . similar
similitudine, la (see-mee-lee-too-dee-neh) . . . . similarity
sincero (seen-cheh-roh) . . . . sincere
sinfonia, la (seen-foh-nee-ah) . . . . symphony
sinistra (see-nee-strah) . . . . left
114 sistema, il (see-steh-mah) . . . . system

sofà, il (soh-fah) . . . . sofa
soggetto, il (soh-jet-toh) . . . . subject
sole, il (soh-leh) . . . . sun
solo (soh-loh) . . . . alone, solitary
somma, la (sohm-mah) . . . . sum, total
sono (soh-noh) . . . . (they) are
sopra (soh-prah) . . . . over, above
   di sopra (dee)(soh-prah) . . . . above, upstairs
soprabito, il (soh-prah-bee-toh) . . . . overcoat
sorella, la (soh-rel-lah) . . . . sister
sorpresa, la (sor-preh-zah) . . . . surprise
sotto (soht-toh) . . . . under, below
   di sotto (dee)(soht-toh) . . . . below, downstairs
sottoveste, la (soht-toh-veh-steh) . . . . slip
Spagna, la (spahn-yah) . . . . Spain
spagnolo, lo (spahn-yoh-loh) . . . . Spanish, Spaniard
spazzolino da denti, lo (spah-tsoh-lee-noh)(dah)(den-tee) . . .
. . . . toothbrush
specchio, lo (spek-kee-oh) . . . . mirror
spesso (spes-soh) . . . . often
spettacolo, lo (spet-tah-koh-loh) . . . . spectacle, show
spingere (speen-jeh-reh) . . . . to push (doors)
sportello, lo (spor-tel-loh) . . . . ticket window, counter
stagioni, le (stah-joh-nee) . . . . seasons
stanco (stahn-koh) . . . . tired
stanza, la (stahn-zah) . . . . room
stanza da bagno, la (stahn-zah)(dah)(bahn-yoh) . bathroom
Stati Uniti, gli (stah-tee)(oo-nee-tee) . . . . . United States
stazione dei treni, la (stah-tsee-oh-neh)(deh-ee)(treh-nee) . . .
. . . . train station
stazione di benzina, la (stah-tsee-oh-neh)(dee)(ben-tsee-nah)
. . . . gas station
stivali, gli (stee-vah-lee) . . . . boots
strada, la (strah-dah) . . . . street
straniero, lo (strah-nee-eh-roh) . . . . stranger, foreigner
straordinario (strah-or-dee-nah-ree-oh) . . . . . extraordinary
studio, lo (stoo-dee-oh) . . . . study, studio
su (soo) . . . . on
successo, il (soo-ches-soh) . . . . success
succo, il (soo-koh) . . . . juice
sud, il (sood) . . . . south
Sudafrica, il (sood-ah-free-kah) . . . . South Africa
sul (sool) . . . . on the
sulla (sool-lah) . . . . on the
Suo (soo-oh) . . . . your
superiore (soo-peh-ree-oh-reh) . . . . superior, above
supermercato, il (soo-pair-mair-kah-toh) . . . . supermarket
sveglia, la (zvel-yah) . . . . alarm clock
Svizzera, la (zveet-tsair-ah) . . . . Switzerland

T

tabaccheria, la (tah-bahk-keh-ree-ah) . . . . tobacco shop
tabacco, il (tah-bahk-koh) . . . . tobacco
taglia, la (tahl-yah) . . . . size
tappeto, il (tahp-peh-toh) . . . . carpet
tariffa, la (tah-reef-fah) . . . . fare
tassa, la (tahs-sah) . . . . tax
tassì, il (tahs-see) . . . . taxi
tavola calda, la (tah-voh-lah)(kahl-dah) . . . . cafeteria
tavolo, il (tah-voh-loh) . . . . table
tazza, la (tah-tsah) . . . . cup
tè, il (teh) . . . . tea
teatro, il (teh-ah-troh) . . . . theater
tedesco, il (teh-deh-skoh) . . . . German
telefono, il (teh-leh-foh-noh) . . . . telephone
telefonata, la (teh-leh-foh-nah-tah) . . . . telephone call

telefonata interurbana, la *(teh-leh-foh-nah-tah)(een-tair-oor-bah-nah)* . . . . long-distance call
telegramma, il *(teh-leh-grahm-mah)* . . . . telegram
televisore, il *(teh-leh-vee-zoh-reh)* . . . . television
temperatura, la *(tem-peh-rah-too-rah)* . . . . temperature
tempo, il *(tem-poh)* . . . . weather, time
tendina, la *(ten-dee-nah)* . . . . curtain
termometro, il *(tair-moh-meh-troh))* . . . . thermometer
terrazza, la *(tair-rah-tsah)* . . . . terrace
tesoro, il *(teh-zoh-roh)* . . . . treasure
tintoria, la *(teen-toh-ree-ah)* . . . . dry cleaner's
tipiche *(tee-pee-keh)* . . . . typical
tirare *(tee-rah-reh)* . . . . to pull (doors)
titolo, il *(tee-toh-loh)* . . . . title
torre, la *(tor-reh)* . . . . tower
   La Torre Pendente *(tor-reh)(pen-den-teh)* . . . .
    . . . . Leaning Tower of Pisa
tovagliolo, il *(toh-vahl-yoh-loh)* . . . . napkin
tram, il *(trahm)* . . . . tram, street car
tranquillo *(trahn-kweel-loh)* . . . . calm, tranquil
trattoria, la *(traht-toh-ree-ah)* . . . . restaurant
travel check, i *(trah-vel)(check)* . . . . . . traveler's checks
tre *(treh)* . . . . three
tredici *(treh-dee-chee)* . . . . thirteen
treno, il *(treh-noh)* . . . . train
trenta *(tren-tah)* . . . . thirty
trovare *(troh-vah-reh)* . . . . to find
tu *(too)* . . . . you (informal/singular)
Tunisia, la *(too-nee-zee-ah)* . . . . Tunisia
Turchia, la *(toor-kee-ah)* . . . . Turkey
turista, il *(too-ree-stah)* . . . . tourist
tutto *(toot-toh)* . . . . everything

U

ufficio, l' *(oof-fee-choh)* . . . . office
ufficio oggetti smarriti, l' *(oof-fee-choh)(oh-jet-tee)(zmar-ree-tee)* . . . . lost-and-found office
ufficio di cambio, l' *(oof-fee-choh)(dee)(kahm-bee-oh)* . . . .
    . . . . money-exchange office
ufficio postale, l' *(oof-fee-choh)(poh-stah-leh)* . . . . post office
ultimo *(ool-tee-moh)* . . . . last, ultimate, final
un, un' *(oon)* . . . . a
un po' *(oon)(poh)* . . . . a little
una *(oo-nah)* . . . . a
unico *(oo-nee-koh)* . . . . unique, only, single
   senso unico *(sen-soh)(oo-nee-koh)* . . . . . . one-way (traffic)
undici *(oon-dee-chee)* . . . . eleven
Ungheria, la *(oon-gair-ee-ah)* . . . . Hungary
universale *(oo-nee-vair-sah-leh)* . . . . universal
università, l' *(oo-nee-vair-see-tah)* . . . . university
uno *(oo-noh)* . . . . one, a
uova, le *(oo-oh-vah)* . . . . eggs
urbano *(oor-bah-noh)* . . . . urban
usato *(oo-zah-toh)* . . . . used, second-hand
uscire *(oo-shee-reh)* . . . . to go out, to exit
uscita, l' *(oo-shee-tah)* . . . . exit
uscita di sicurezza, l' *(oo-shee-tah)(dee)(see-koo-reh-tsah)* . .
    . . . . emergency exit
usi *(oo-zee)* . . . . use
usuale *(oo-zoo-ah-leh)* . . . . usual, customary
utensile, l' *(oo-ten-see-leh)* . . . . utensil

V

vacanze, le *(vah-kahn-tseh)* . . . . vacation
vaccinazione, la *(vah-chee-nah-tsee-oh-neh)* . . . . vaccination
vagone letto, il *(vah-goh-neh)(let-toh)* . . . . sleeping car

vagone ristorante, il *(vah-goh-neh)(ree-stoh-rahn-teh)* . . . . .
    . . . . dining car
valigia, la *(vah-lee-jah)* . . . . suitcase
vaniglia, la *(vah-neel-yah)* . . . . vanilla
vaporetto, il *(vah-poh-ret-toh)* . . . . . . steam ferry (in Venice)
varietà, la *(vah-ree-eh-tah)* . . . . variety
vaso, il *(vah-zoh)* . . . . vase
vecchio *(vek-kee-oh)* . . . . old
vedere *(veh-deh-reh)* . . . . to see
veloce *(veh-loh-cheh)* . . . . fast
vena, la *(veh-nah)* . . . . vein
vendere *(ven-deh-reh)* . . . . to sell
venditore, il *(ven-dee-toh-reh)* . . . . vendor, seller
venerdì *(veh-nair-dee)* . . . . Friday
vengo *(ven-goh)* . . . . I come
venire *(veh-nee-reh)* . . . . to come
venti *(ven-tee)* . . . . twenty
vento, il *(ven-toh)* . . . . windy
verbo, il *(vair-boh)* . . . . verb
verde *(vair-deh)* . . . . green
verdura, la *(vair-doo-rah)* . . . . vegetable
vergine, la *(vair-jee-neh)* . . . . virgin
vero *(veh-roh)* . . . . true, real
versione, la *(vair-zee-oh-neh)* . . . . version
vestiti, i *(veh-stee-tee)* . . . . clothing
vestito, il *(veh-stee-toh)* . . . . dress
via *(vee-ah)* . . . . by
   via aerea *(vee-ah)(ah-eh-reh-ah)* . . . . by airmail
via, la *(vee-ah)* . . . . way
viaggiare *(vee-ah-jah-reh)* . . . . to travel
viaggiatore, il *(vee-ah-jah-toh-reh)* . . . . traveler
viaggio, il *(vee-ah-joh)* . . . . trip
viene *(vee-eh-neh)* . . . . come, comes
vietato *(vee-eh-tah-toh)* . . . . prohibited
   vietato entrare *(vee-eh-tah-toh)(en-trah-reh)* . . . do not enter
vigoroso *(vee-goh-roh-zoh)* . . . . vigorous
vino, il *(vee-noh)* . . . . wine
violetto *(vee-oh-let-toh)* . . . . violet
visita, la *(vee-zee-tah)* . . . . visit
   fare una vista *(fah-reh)(oo-nah)(vee-zee-tah)* . . to pay a visit
visitare *(vee-zee-tah-reh)* . . . . to visit
vita, la *(vee-tah)* . . . . life
vitamina, la *(vee-tah-mee-nah)* . . . . vitamin
vitello, il *(vee-tel-loh)* . . . . veal
voi *(voy)* . . . . you (plural)
volere *(voh-leh-reh)* . . . . to want
volo, il *(voh-loh)* . . . . flight
vorrei *(vor-reh-ee)* . . . . I would like
vorremmo *(vor-rem-moh)* . . . . we would like

W

W.C., il *(vee-chee)* . . . . toilet, water closet

Z

zero *(zeh-roh)* . . . . zero
zia, la *(dzee-ah)* . . . . aunt
zio, lo *(dzee-oh)* . . . . uncle
zodiaco, lo *(zoh-dee-ah-koh)* . . . . zodiac
zona, la *(zoh-nah)* . . . . zone
zoo, lo *(dzoh)* . . . . zoo
zuppa, la *(zoop-pah)* . . . . soup

Did you have fun learning your new language? We at Bilingual Books hope you enjoy your travels wherever they might take you!

This beverage guide is intended to explain the variety of beverages available to you while **in Italia.** It is by no means complete. Some of the experimenting has been left up to you, but this should get you started.

BEVANDE CALDE (hot drinks)

caffè . . . . coffee (espresso)
caffellatte . . . . coffee with steamed milk
cappuccino . . . . coffee with steamed milk and milk froth
caffè americano . . . . American-style coffee
caffè macchiato . . . . coffee with a little milk or cream
cioccolata . . . . cocoa

tè . . . . tea
tè con limone . . . . tea with lemon
tè con latte . . . . tea with milk

BEVANDE FREDDE (cold drinks)

latte freddo . . . . cold milk
frappé . . . . milkshake
succo . . . . juice
succo di arancia . . . . orange juice
acqua . . . . water
acqua minerale . . . . mineral water
amarena . . . . cherry syrup drink
orzata . . . . almond syrup drink
tè freddo . . . . iced tea
caffè freddo . . . . iced coffee
ghiaccio . . . . ice

VINO (wine)

There is a wide variety of wines in Italy. Each region produces its own wine, ranging in taste from very sweet to very dry. You may drink wine by the **bicchiere** (glass), **litro** (liter), **mezzo litro** (half liter), or the **bottiglia** (bottle).

vino rosso . . . . red wine
vino bianco . . . . white wine
vino rosè . . . . rosé wine
spumante . . . . sparkling wine

vino ordinario . . . . . . table wine
vino da tavola . . . . . . table wine
vino della casa . . . . . . house wine
vino locale . . . . local wine of the region
dolce . . . . sweet
amabile . . . . between sweet and dry
secco . . . . dry

BIRRA (beer)

There are many brands of beer. **Birra** is generally purchased **in bottiglia** (bottled) or **alla spina** (draught).

BEVANDE ALCOOLICHE (alcoholic beverages)

vodka . . . . vodka
whisky . . . . scotch
bourbon . . . . bourbon
gin . . . . gin
rum . . . . rum
martini dry . . . . American martini
acquavite . . . . natural grain spirits
grappa . . . . wine brandy
cognac . . . . cognac

Il Menù

Preparazione (preparation)

cotto	cooked
crudo	raw
arrosto	roasted
fritto	fried
al forno	baked
alla griglia, ai ferri	grilled
allo spiedo	roasted on a spit
bollito	boiled
affumicato	smoked
alla brace	charcoal-broiled
farcito	stuffed
al sangue	rare
al punto	medium
ben cotto	well-done

Altri (others)

marmellata	jam
miele	honey
sale	salt
pepe	pepper
olio	oil
aceto	vinegar
senape/mostarda	mustard
riso	rice
pane	bread
formaggio	cheese
dolci	desserts
torta	cake
dolce	pastry
gelato	ice cream
panna montata	whipped cream

Riso, Risotto (rice)

alla milanese	with saffron
con funghi	with mushrooms
alla marinara	tomato sauce, clams, prawns

Frutta (fruit)

mela	apple
pera	pear
pesca	peach
banana	banana
arancia	orange
mandarino	tangerine
ciliegie	cherries
cocomero	watermelon
prugna	plum
uva	grapes
uva passa	raisins
dattero	date
limone	lemon
ananas	pineapple
pompelmo	grapefruit
fichi	figs
fragole	strawberries
lamponi	raspberries
mirtilli	blueberries

Bevande (beverages)

birra	beer
latte	milk
caffè	coffee
caffellatte	coffee with steamed milk
succo di . . .	juice of . . .
limonata	lemonade
acqua minerale	bottled mineral water
vino rosso	red wine
vino bianco	white wine
vino rosè	rosé wine

(bwohn) **Buon appetito!** *(ahp-peh-tee-toh)*
enjoy your meal

Pastasciutta (pasta)

spaghetti	long, solid-core pasta
fettucine	flat noodle
ravioli	small, stuffed pasta square
lasagne	baked, layered casserole
cannelloni	stuffed cylinder-shaped pasta
tortellini	small stuffed pasta
vermicelli	very thin pasta
cannolo	short tubes of macaroni
cappelletti	round, cap-shaped pasta
conchiglie	shell-shaped pasta
gnocchi	small dumplings
linguine	narrow, flat noodles
penne	hollow pasta, cut diagonally
rigatoni	large, hollow pasta

Verdura (vegetables)

cipolle	onions
piselli	green peas
pomodori	tomatoes
fagiolini	string beans
cavolfiore	cauliflower
carciofo	artichokes
carote	carrots
asparagi	asparagus
spinaci	spinach
lenticchie	lentils
funghi	mushrooms
broccoli	broccoli
melanzane	eggplant
olive	olives
patate	potatoes
peperoni	bell peppers
prezzemolo	parsley
rapanelli	radishes
sedano	celery
zucca	yellow squash
zucchini	zucchini

Minestre e Zuppe (soups)

minestrone	thick vegetable soup
minestrina	thin clear broth
zuppa di pesce	fish soup
stracciatella	broth with beaten eggs and Parmesan cheese
pavese	broth with poached egg on fried bread

Antipasti (appetizers)

acciughe	anchovies
di mare	seafood with lemon-juice dressing
misto	mixed appetizers
frutti di mare	seafood
gamberi	shrimps and prawns
lumache	snails
ostriche	oysters
peperonata	sliced peppers, onions and tomatoes
mortadella	bologna
prosciutto	ham
salame	variety of sausages
salsicce	cooked sausage

Insalate (salads)

verde	tossed green salad
capricciosa	mixed vegetables, with ham in mayonnaise sauce
di pesce	boiled fish
di riso	cold rice, vegetables, seafood, mayonnaise
mista	mixed green salad with tomatoes
viennese	tuna, hard-boiled eggs, beans, olives

Carne (meat)

Vitello (veal)

bistecca di vitello	loin veal steak
costoletta di vitello	veal chop or steak
coteletta	veal steak without bone
alla Milanese	breaded veal cutlets
lombata di vitello	loin of veal
noce di vitello	sirloin of veal
rollatine di vitello	rolled stuffed breast of veal
spalla di vitello al forno	roast shoulder of veal

Maiale (pork)

arrosto di maiale	roast loin of pork
arrostino alla salvia	roast pork with sage
arrosto di porchetta	stuffed roast suckling pig
zampe di maiale	pig's feet

FOLD HERE

Manzo (beef)

Italian	English
braciola	rib steak
entrecote	boneless rib steak
fegato	liver
cervella	brains
lingua di bue	beef tongue
stracotto	stew

Agnello (lamb)

abbacchio	milk-fed lamb
bracciolette d'abbacchio	grilled lamb chops or cutlets
abbacchio al forno	roasted lamb
costole alla Milanese	fried breaded lamb chops
tracciole d'agnello	a type of shish kebab

Pollame (poultry)

Italian	English
pollo	chicken
tacchino	turkey
faraona	guinea fowl
cappone	capon
piccione	pigeon
quaglie	quail
fagiano	pheasant

Cacciagione (wild game)

anatra	duck
cervo	deer
coniglio	rabbit
lepre	hare
tordo	thrush

Pesci e Frutti di Mare (fish and seafood)

acciughe	anchovies
aragosta	lobster
calamari	squid
gamberi	shrimp or prawns
granchio	crab
merluzzo	codfish
cozze	mussels
persico	perch
pesce spada	swordfish
polipo	octopus
salmone	salmon
sardine	sardines
sogliola	sole
spigola	sea bass
storione	sturgeon
tonno	tuna
trota	trout
vongole	clams

FOLD HERE

Sugo di Carne (meat sauces)

alla Bolognese	meat and tomato sauce
alla Romagnola	tomato sauce with garlic and parsley
alla carbonara	sauce of eggs, bacon and garlic
alla Fiorentina	herbal meat sauce with green peas
all'arrabbiata	herbal tomato sauce of bacon, sausage and cayenne
alla Piemontese	herbal meat sauce with nutmeg and truffles
alla Romana	seasoned meat sauce

Senza Carne (meatless sauces)

aglio e olio	olive oil and garlic
alla besciamella	creamed white sauce
al burro	butter and Parmesan
alla Campagnola	mushrooms, tomatoes and herbs
alla crema	white sauce with egg yolk and Parmesan cheese
al pesto	basil, garlic and pine nuts
alla Napolitana	tomatoes, basil and Parmesan cheese
al pomodoro	herbal tomato sauce

Frutti di Mare (seafood sauces)

alla boscaiola	tuna, anchovies, tomatoes and mushrooms
ai frutti di mare	herbs, tomatoes and seafood
al tonno	tuna, garlic, tomatoes and capers
di magro	tuna, anchovies and herbs
alla posillipo	herbs, tomatoes and seafood
alle vongole	clams and garlic, with or without tomatoes

(ee-oh)
io

(noy)
noi

(loo-ee)
lui

(leh-ee)
Lei

(leh-ee)
lei

(loh-roh)
loro

(par-lah-reh)
parlare

(par-loh)
io parlo

(or-dee-nah-reh)
ordinare

(or-dee-noh)
io ordino

(eem-pah-rah-reh)
imparare

(eem-pah-roh)
io imparo

(ah-bee-tah-reh)
abitare

(ah-bee-toh)
io abito

(kohm-prah-reh)
comprare

(kohm-proh)
io compro

(kee-ah-mar-see)
chiamarsi

(mee) *(kee-ah-moh)*
io mi chiamo

we	I
you	he
they	she
to order	to speak
I order	I speak
to live/reside	to learn
I live/reside	I learn
to be called	to buy
my name is . . .	I buy

(veh-nee-reh)
venire

(ven-goh)
io vengo

(ahn-dah-reh)
andare

(vah-doh)
io vado

(ah-veh-reh)
avere

(oh)
io ho

(ah-veh-reh) *(bee-zohn-yoh)* *(dee)*
avere bisogno di

(oh) *(bee-zohn-yoh)* *(dee)*
io ho bisogno di

(dee-reh)
dire

(dee-koh)
io dico

(vor-reh-ee)
vorrei

(mahn-jah-reh)
mangiare

(mahn-joh)
io mangio

(beh-reh)
bere

(beh-voh)
io bevo

(troh-vah-reh)
trovare

(troh-voh)
io trovo

(kah-pee-reh)
capire

(kah-pee-skoh)
io capisco

(ven-deh-reh)
vendere

(ven-doh)
io vendo

(ree-peh-teh-reh)
ripetere

(ree-peh-toh)
io ripeto

to go	to come
I go	I come
to have need of/need	to have
I need	I have
I would like	to say
	I say
to drink	to eat
I drink	I eat
to understand	to find
I understand	I find
to repeat	to sell
I repeat	I sell

(veh-deh-reh)
vedere

(veh-doh)
io vedo

(fah-reh)
fare

(fah-choh)
io faccio

(mahn-dah-reh)
mandare

(mahn-doh)
io mando

(dor-mee-reh)
dormire

(dor-moh)
io dormo

(ah-spet-tah-reh)
aspettare

(ah-spet-toh)
io aspetto

(leh-jeh-reh)
leggere

(leh-goh)
io leggo

(mee) *(dee-ah)*
mi dia . . .

(skree-veh-reh)
scrivere

(skree-voh)
io scrivo

(pah-gah-reh)
pagare

(pah-goh)
io pago

(poh-teh-reh)
potere

(pohs-soh)
io posso

(doh-veh-reh)
dovere

(deh-voh)
io devo

(sah-peh-reh)
sapere

(soh)
io so

to do/make	to see
I do/make	I see
to sleep	to send
I sleep	I send
to read	to wait (for)
I read	I wait (for)
to write	give me . . .
I write	
to be able to/can	to pay (for)
I can	I pay (for)
to know (fact)	to have to/must/to owe
I know	I have to/must/owe

(preh-noh-tah-reh)
prenotare

(preh-noh-toh)
io prenoto

(ahn-dah-reh)   *(ah-eh-reh-oh)*
andare in aereo

(vah-doh)   *(ah-eh-reh-oh)*
io vado in aereo

(vee-ah-jah-reh)
viaggiare

(vee-ah-joh)
io viaggio

(par-tee-reh)
partire

(par-toh)
io parto

(ar-ree-vah-reh)
arrivare

(ar-ree-voh)
io arrivo

(kahm-bee-ah-reh)
cambiare

(kahm-bee-oh)
io cambio

(fah-reh)   *(leh)*   *(vah-lee-jeh)*
fare le valigie

(fah-choh)   *(vah-lee-jeh)*
io faccio le valigie

(gwee-dah-reh)
guidare

(gwee-doh)
io guido

(cheh)   *(chee)*   *(soh-noh)*
c'è / ci sono

(leh-ee)   *(ah)*
Lei ha . . . ?

(lah-vah-reh)
lavare

(lah-voh)
io lavo

(pair-deh-reh)
perdere

(pair-doh)
io perdo

to fly	to reserve/book
I fly	I reserve/book
to leave	to travel
I leave	I travel
to transfer (vehicles) /to change money	to arrive
I transfer/change money	I arrive
to drive	to pack
I drive	I pack
Do you have . . . ?	there is/there are
to lose	to wash
I lose	I wash

(oh-jee)
oggi

(koh-meh)   *(vah)*
Come va?

(ee-eh-ree)
ieri

(pair)   *(fah-voh-reh)*
per favore

(doh-mah-nee)
domani

(grah-tsee-eh)
grazie

(chow)
ciao

(mee)   *(skoo-zee)*
mi scusi

(vek-kee-oh)   *(noo-oh-voh)*
vecchio - nuovo

(kwahn-toh)   *(koh-stah)*
Quanto costa?

(grahn-deh)   *(peek-koh-loh)*
grande - piccolo

(ah-pair-toh)   *(kee-oo-zoh)*
aperto - chiuso

How are you?	today
please	yesterday
thank you	tomorrow
excuse me	hi/bye
How much does this cost?	old - new
open - closed	large - small

(mah-lah-toh)   *(bwoh-nah)*   *(sah-loo-teh)*
malato - in buona salute

(bwoh-noh)   *(kaht-tee-voh)*
buono - cattivo

(kahl-doh)   *(fred-doh)*
caldo - freddo

(kor-toh)   *(loon-goh)*
corto - lungo

(ahl-toh)   *(bahs-soh)*
alto - basso

(soh-prah)   *(soht-toh)*
sopra - sotto

(see-nee-strah)   *(deh-strah)*
sinistra - destra

(veh-loh-cheh) *(rah-pee-doh)*   *(len-toh)*
veloce/rapido - lento

(vek-kee-oh)   *(joh-vah-neh)*
vecchio - giovane

(eh-koh-noh-mee-koh)   *(kah-roh)*
economico - caro

(poh-veh-roh)   *(reek-koh)*
povero - ricco

(mohl-toh)   *(poh-koh)*
molto - poco

good - bad	ill - healthy
short - long	hot - cold
above - below	tall - short
fast - slow	left - right
inexpensive-expensive	old - young
a lot - a little	poor - rich

Now that you've finished...

You've done it!

You've completed all the Steps, stuck your labels, flashed your cards and cut out your menu guide. Do you realize how far you've come and how much you've learned?

You can now confidently

- ask questions,
- understand directions,
- make reservations,
- order food and
- shop anywhere.

And you can do it all in a foreign language! You can now go anywhere — from a large cosmopolitan restaurant to a small, out-of-the-way village where no one speaks English. Your experiences will be much more enjoyable and worry-free now that you speak the language.

Yes, learning a foreign language can be fun.

Kristine Kershul

Kristine Kershul

Send us this order form with your check, money order or credit card details. If paying by credit card, you may fax your order to **(206) 284-3660** or call us toll-free at **(800) 488-5068**. All prices are in US dollars and are subject to change without notice.

Modulo di Ordinazione
order form

10 minutes a day Series	QTY.	PRICE	TOTAL
ARABIC *in 10 minutes a day*®		$19.95	
CHINESE *in 10 minutes a day*®		$19.95	
FRENCH *in 10 minutes a day*®		$19.95	
GERMAN *in 10 minutes a day*®		$19.95	
HEBREW *in 10 minutes a day*®		$19.95	
INGLÉS *en 10 minutos al día*®		$19.95	
ITALIAN *in 10 minutes a day*®		$19.95	
JAPANESE *in 10 minutes a day*®		$17.95	
NORWEGIAN *in 10 minutes a day*®		$19.95	
PORTUGUESE *in 10 minutes a day*®		$18.95	
RUSSIAN *in 10 minutes a day*®		$19.95	
SPANISH *in 10 minutes a day*®		$18.95	
10 minutes a day AUDIO	QTY.	PRICE	TOTAL
FRENCH *in 10 minutes a day*® AUDIO		$59.95	
FRENCH AUDIO CDs only *(no book)*		$42.95	
ITALIAN *in 10 minutes a day*® AUDIO		$59.95	
ITALIAN AUDIO CDs only *(no book)*		$42.95	
SPANISH *in 10 minutes a day*® AUDIO		$59.95	
SPANISH AUDIO CDs only *(no book)*		$42.95	
Language Map Series	QTY.	PRICE	TOTAL
ARABIC *a language map*®		$7.95	
CHINESE *a language map*®		$7.95	
FRENCH *a language map*®		$7.95	
GERMAN *a language map*®		$7.95	
GREEK *a language map*®		$7.95	
HAWAIIAN *a language map*®		$7.95	
HEBREW *a language map*®		$7.95	
INGLÉS *un mapa del lenguaje*®		$7.95	
ITALIAN *a language map*®		$7.95	
JAPANESE *a language map*®		$7.95	
NORWEGIAN *a language map*®		$7.95	
POLISH *a language map*®		$7.95	
PORTUGUESE *a language map*®		$7.95	
RUSSIAN *a language map*®		$7.95	
SPANISH *a language map*®		$7.95	
VIETNAMESE *a language map*®		$7.95	

† For delivery to individuals in Washington State, you must add 8.8% sales tax on the item total and the shipping costs combined. If your order is being delivered outside Washington State, you do not need to add sales tax.	Item Total
	* Shipping +
	Total
	† Sales Tax +
	ORDER TOTAL

Name _____

Address _____

_____

City _____ State _____ Zip _____

Day Phone (_____)_____

❑ My check or money order for $_____ is enclosed.
   Please make checks and money orders payable to Bilingual Books, Inc.

❑ Bill my credit card ❑ VISA ❑ MC ❑ AMEX
   No. _____ Exp. date ____/____
   Signature _____

**Bilingual Books, Inc. • 1719 West Nickerson Street
Seattle, WA 98119 USA**

10 minutes a day® AUDIO

by Kristine K. Kershul

The *10 minutes a day*® AUDIO is based on the immensely successful *10 minutes a day*® Series. Millions of people around the world have used the *10 minutes a day*® Series for over two decades.

• Eight hours of personal instruction on six CDs.

• Use the CDs in combination with the companion book, and maximize your progress as you see AND hear the language.

• Listen to native speakers and practice right along with them.

• Suitable for the classroom, the homeschooler, as well as business and leisure travelers.

• The CDs in the *10 minutes a day*® AUDIO may also be purchased separately from the *10 minutes a day*® books.

Language Map® Series

by Kristine K. Kershul

These handy *Language Maps*® provide the essential words and phrases to cover the basics for any trip.

• Over 1,000 essential words and phrases divided into convenient categories.

• Laminated , folding design allows for quicker reference while resisting spills, tearing, and damage from frequent use.

• Durable, to hold up to being sat on, dropped, and stuffed into backpacks, pockets, and purses.

• An absolute must for anyone traveling abroad or studying at home.

For a list of available languages and ordering information, please see the order form on the previous page.